THE UNIVERSE AND OUR PLACE IN IT

ASTEROIDS, METEORS, METEORITES, AND COMETS

Edited by
Nicholas Faulkner and Erik Gregersen

Britannica®
Educational Publishing

IN ASSOCIATION WITH

ROSEN
EDUCATIONAL SERVICES

Published in 2019 by Britannica Educational Publishing (a trademark of Encyclopædia Britannica, Inc.) in association with The Rosen Publishing Group, Inc.
29 East 21st Street, New York, NY 10010

Distributed exclusively by Rosen Publishing.
To see additional Britannica Educational Publishing titles, go to rosenpublishing.com.

Britannica Educational Publishing
J.E. Luebering: Executive Director, Core Editorial
Andrea R. Field: Managing Editor, Compton's by Britannica

Rosen Publishing
Nicholas Faulkner: Editor
Brian Garvey: Series Designer / Book Layout
Cindy Reiman: Photography Manager
Nicole DiMella: Photo Researcher

Library of Congress Cataloging-in-Publication Data

Names: Faulkner, Nicholas, editor. | Gregersen, Erik, editor.
Title: Asteroids, meteors, meteorites, and comets / edited by Nicholas Faulkner and Erik Gregersen.
Description: New York : Britannica Educational Publishing, in Association with Rosen Educational Services, 2019 | Series: The universe and our place in it | Includes bibliographical references and index. | Audience: Grades 7–12.
Identifiers: LCCN 2018008352| ISBN 9781680488746 (library bound) | ISBN 9781680488739 (pbk.)
Subjects: LCSH: Asteroids—Juvenile literature. | Meteors—Juvenile literature. | Comets—Juvenile literature.
Classification: LCC QB377 .A88 2018 | DDC 523.4—dc23
LC record available at https://lccn.loc.gov/2018008352

Manufactured in the United States of America

CONTENTS

CHAPTER 3

S ometimes one can see a flash of light streak across the night sky and disappear. This is commonly called a shooting star, though they are not stars. They are small chunks of stone, metal, or other materials that orbit the Sun. Sometimes they enter Earth's atmosphere and the friction generated by their great speed causes them to burn up. The fragments may either vaporize before traveling far or actually hit the ground.

These objects have different names depending on their location. One that is beyond Earth's atmosphere is called a meteoroid. A meteoroid that enters Earth's atmosphere is called a meteor. A meteor that actually lands on Earth's surface is called a meteorite.

Meteorites, which are sturdy enough to reach the ground, are mostly pieces of asteroids, or huge rocks that orbit the Sun. Comets, on the other hand, are flimsy objects made mostly of frozen water, frozen gases, and some gritty material. They also orbit the Sun.

Meteoroids vary from small rocks to boulders weighing a ton or more. A relative few have orbits that bring them into Earth's atmosphere and down to the surface as meteorites. Most meteorites that have been collected on Earth are probably from

Comet Siding Spring appears to streak across the sky like a super-hero in this infrared image from NASA's Wide-field Infrared Survey Explorer, or WISE.

asteroids. A few have been identified as being from the Moon, Mars, or the asteroid Vesta.

Most meteoroids that enter the atmosphere heat up sufficiently to glow and appear as meteors, and the great majority of these vaporize completely or break up before they reach the surface. Some meteorites contain microscopic crystals whose isotopic proportions are unique and appear to be dust grains that formed in the atmospheres of different stars.

Most meteors that burn up in Earth's atmosphere are tiny dustlike particles, the remains of disintegrated comets. Sometimes a swarm of meteoroids enters Earth's atmosphere, causing a meteor shower, with tens or hundreds of shooting stars flashing across the sky in less than an hour. Virtually all these meteors burn up in the upper atmosphere.

More than 500,000 asteroids with well-established orbits are known, and thousands of additional objects are discovered each year. Hundreds of thousands more have been seen, but their orbits have not been as well determined. It is estimated that several million asteroids exist, but most are small, and their combined mass is estimated to be less than a thousandth that of Earth.

Many comets have been observed over the centuries. Comets are considered to come from a vast reservoir, the Oort cloud, orbiting the Sun and containing trillions of icy objects with the potential to become active comets. Most make only a single pass through the inner solar system, but some are deflected by Jupiter or Saturn into orbits that allow them to return at predictable times. Halley's Comet is the best known of these periodic comets, whose next return into the inner solar system is predicted for 2061.

Many short-period comets are thought to come from the Kuiper belt, a region lying beyond Neptune's orbit, but including part of Pluto's, and housing perhaps hundreds of millions of comet nuclei. Very few comet masses have been well determined, but most are probably one-billionth the mass of Earth.

As scientists develop new technologies, they can more closely study these celestial bodies and gain insight into the formation of our solar system. By understanding what these bodies are composed of, researchers can better understand how the solar system originated and has evolved.

CHAPTER 1

AMAZING ASTEROIDS

Asteroids are small, rocky bodies that orbit, or travel around, the Sun. In general, they are materials left over from the formation of planets or are created when other bodies in space collide and break apart.

Most of the rocky asteroids move around the Sun in elliptical orbits in the same direction of the Sun's rotation. Such motion is termed "prograde." Looking down on the solar system from a vantage point above Earth's North Pole, an observer would find that prograde orbits are counterclockwise. Orbits in a clockwise direction are called retrograde.

Between the orbits of Mars and Jupiter are a host of asteroids, about 1,000 km (600 miles) or less in diameter, that orbit in the nearby ring called the asteroid belt. Many astronomers consider the asteroid belt a demarcation point between the inner solar system (consisting mainly of the terrestrial planets) and the outer solar system. It is because of their small size and large numbers relative to the major planets that asteroids are also called minor planets. The two designations have been used interchangeably, though the term "asteroid" is more widely recognized by the general public. Among scientists, those who study individual objects with dynamically interesting orbits or groups of objects with similar orbital characteristics generally use the term "minor planet," whereas those who study the physical properties of such objects usually refer to them as "asteroids."

EARLY OBSERVATIONS

The first asteroid was discovered on January 1, 1801, by the astronomer Giuseppe Piazzi at Palermo, Italy. At first Piazzi thought that he had discovered a comet. However, after the orbital elements of the object had been computed, it became clear that the object moved in a planetlike orbit between the orbits of Mars and Jupiter. Owing to illness, Piazzi was able to observe the object only until February 11. Although the discovery was reported in the press, Piazzi only shared details of his observations with a few astronomers at first and did not publish a complete set of his observations until months later. The short arc of observations did not allow computation of an orbit of sufficient accuracy to predict where the object would reappear when it moved back into the night sky.

Giuseppe Piazzi.

There matters might have stood were it not for astronomers searching for a "missing" planet between Mars and Jupiter during an astronomical conference in 1796. (Unfortunately, Piazzi was not a party to this attempt to locate the missing planet.) In 1801, German mathematician Carl Friedrich Gauss developed a method for computing the orbit of an asteroid from only a few observations. Using Gauss's predictions, the German Hungarian astronomer Franz von Zach rediscovered Piazzi's "lost" object on January 1, 1802. Piazzi named this object Ceres after the ancient Roman grain goddess and patron goddess of Sicily, thereby initiating a tradition that continues to the present day—asteroids are named by their discoverers.

The discovery of three more faint objects (at least when compared with Mars and Jupiter) in similar orbits over the next six years—Pallas, Juno, and Vesta—complicated this elegant solution to the missing-planet problem and gave rise to the surprisingly long-lived though no longer accepted idea that the asteroids were remnants of a planet that had exploded. Following this flurry of activity, the search for the planet appears to have been abandoned until 1830, when Karl L. Hencke renewed it. In 1845 he discovered a fifth asteroid, which he named Astraea.

There were 88 known asteroids by 1866, when the next major discovery was made: Daniel Kirkwood, an American astronomer, noted that there were gaps (now known as Kirkwood gaps) in the distribution of asteroid distances from the Sun. The introduction of photography to the search for new asteroids in 1891, by which time 322 asteroids had been identified, accelerated the discovery rate. The asteroid designated (323) Brucia, detected in 1891, was the first to be discovered by means of photography. By the end of the 19th century, 464 had been found; this grew to more than 100,000 by the end of the 20th century and to more than seven times that number by 2018. This explosive growth was a spin-off of a survey designed to find 90 percent of asteroids with diameters greater than 1 km (0.6 miles) that can cross Earth's orbit and thus have the potential to collide with the planet.

LATER ADVANCES

During much of the 19th century, most discoveries concerning asteroids were based on studies of their orbits. The vast majority of knowledge about the physical characteristics of asteroids—for example, their size, shape, rotation period, composition, mass, and density—was learned beginning in the 20th century, in particular since the 1970s. As a result of such studies, these objects went from being merely "minor" planets to becoming small worlds in their own right.

This artist's concept illustrates catastrophic collisions between asteroids in the belt between Mars and Jupiter and how they have formed families of objects on similar orbits around the Sun.

In 1918 the Japanese astronomer Hirayama Kiyotsugu recognized clustering in three of the orbital elements (semimajor axis, eccentricity, and inclination) of various asteroids. He speculated that objects sharing these elements had been formed by explosions of larger parent asteroids, and he called such groups of asteroids "families."

In the mid-20th century, calculations of the lifetimes of asteroids whose orbits passed close to those of the major planets showed that most such asteroids were destined either to collide with a planet or to be ejected from the solar system on timescales of a few hundred thousand to a few million years. Since the age of the solar system is approximately 4.6 billion years, this meant that the asteroids seen today in such orbits must have entered them recently and implied that there was a source for these asteroids. At first this source was thought to be comets that had been captured by the planets and that had lost their volatile material through repeated passages inside the orbit of Mars. It is now known that most such objects come from regions in the main asteroid belt near Kirkwood gaps and other orbital resonances.

NAMING ASTEROIDS

Because of their widespread occurrence, asteroids are assigned numbers as well as names. The numbers are assigned consecutively after accurate orbital elements have been determined. Ceres is officially known as (1) Ceres, Pallas as (2) Pallas, and so forth. Of the more than 760,000 asteroids discovered by 2017, about 68 percent were numbered. Asteroid discoverers have the right to choose names for their discoveries as soon as they are numbered. The names selected are submitted to the International Astronomical Union (IAU) for approval.

Prior to the mid-20th century, asteroids were sometimes assigned numbers before accurate orbital elements had been determined, and so some numbered asteroids could not later be located. These objects were referred to as "lost" asteroids. The final lost numbered asteroid, (719) Albert, was recovered in 2000 after a lapse of 89 years. Many newly discovered asteroids still become "lost" because of an insufficiently long span of observations, but no new asteroids are assigned numbers until their orbits are reliably known.

The Minor Planet Center at the Harvard-Smithsonian Center for Astrophysics in Cambridge, Massachusetts, maintains computers for all measurements of asteroid positions. As of 2018, there were more than 188 million such positions in its database.

ASTEROIDS THAT ARE CLOSE TO EARTH

Asteroids that can come close to Earth are called near-Earth asteroids (NEAs), although only some NEAs actually cross Earth's orbit. NEAs are divided into several classes. Asteroids belonging to the class most distant from Earth—those asteroids that can cross the orbit of Mars but that have perihelion distances greater than 1.3 AU—are dubbed Mars crossers. This class is further subdivided into two: shallow Mars crossers (perihelion distances no less than 1.58 AU but less than 1.67 AU) and deep Mars crossers (perihelion distances greater than 1.3 AU but less than 1.58 AU).

The next most distant class of NEAs is the Amors. Members of this group have perihelion distances that are greater than 1.017 AU, which is Earth's aphelion distance, but no greater than 1.3 AU. Amor asteroids therefore do

NEOWISE, the asteroid-hunting portion of the NASA WISE mission, illustrates the differences between orbits of a typical near-Earth asteroid, blue, and a potentially hazardous asteroid, or PHA, orange.

not at present cross Earth's orbit. Because of strong gravitational perturbations produced by their close approaches to Earth, however, the orbital elements of all Earth-approaching asteroids except the shallow Mars crossers change appreciably on timescales as short as years or decades. For this reason, about half the known Amors, including (1221) Amor, the namesake of the group, are part-time Earth crossers. Only asteroids that cross the orbits of planets—i.e., Earth-approaching asteroids and idiosyncratic objects such as (944) Hidalgo and Chiron—suffer significant changes in their orbital elements on timescales shorter than many millions of years.

There are two classes of NEAs that deeply cross Earth's orbit on an almost continuous basis. The first of these to be discovered were the Apollo asteroids, named for (1862) Apollo, which was discovered in 1932 but was lost shortly thereafter and not rediscovered until 1978. The mean distances of Apollo asteroids from the Sun are greater than or equal to 1 AU, and their perihelion distances are less than or equal to Earth's aphelion distance of 1.017 AU; thus, they cross Earth's orbit when near the closest points to the Sun in their own orbits. The other class of Earth-crossing asteroids is named Atens for (2062) Aten, which was discovered in 1976. The Aten asteroids have mean distances from the Sun that are less than 1 AU and aphelion distances that are greater than or equal to 0.983 AU, the perihelion distance of Earth; they cross Earth's orbit when near the farthest points from the Sun of their orbits.

The class of NEAs that was the last to be recognized is composed of asteroids with orbits entirely inside that of Earth. Known as Atira asteroids after (163693) Atira, they have mean distances from the Sun that are less than 1 AU and aphelion distances less than 0.983 AU; they do not cross Earth's orbit.

As of 2018, the known Atira, Aten, Apollo, and Amor asteroids of all sizes numbered 17, 1,342, 8,972, and 7,618, respectively, although these numbers are steadily increasing as the asteroid survey programs progress. Most of these were discovered since 1970, when dedicated searches for these types of asteroids were begun. Astronomers have estimated that there are roughly 50 Atens, 600 Apollos, and 250 Amors that have diameters larger than about 1 km (0.6 miles).

Because they can approach quite close to Earth, some of the best information available on asteroids has come from Earth-based radar studies of NEAs. In 1968 the Apollo asteroid (1566) Icarus became the first NEA to be observed with radar. Some five decades later, over 750 NEAs had been so observed. Because of continuing improvements to the radar systems themselves and to the computers used to process the data, the information provided by this technique increased dramatically beginning in the final decade of the 20th century. For example, the first images of an asteroid, (4769) Castalia, were made using radar data obtained in 1989, more than two years before the first spacecraft flyby of an asteroid—(951) Gaspra by the Galileo spacecraft in 1991. The observations of Castalia provided the first evidence in the solar system for a double-lobed object, interpreted to be two roughly equal-sized bodies in contact. Radar observations of (4179) Toutatis in 1992 revealed it to be several kilometres long with a peanut-shell shape; similar to Castalia, Toutatis appears predominantly to be two components in contact, one about twice as large as the other. The highest-resolution images show craters having diameters between 100 and 600 metres (roughly 300 and 2,000 feet). Radar images of (1620) Geographos obtained in 1994 were numerous enough and of sufficient quality for an animation to be made showing it rotating.

CALCULATING ASTEROID MASS AND DENSITY

Most asteroid masses are low, although present-day observations show that the asteroids measurably perturb the orbits of the major planets. Except for Mars, however, these perturbations are too small to allow the masses of the asteroids in question to be determined. Radio-ranging measurements that were transmitted from the surface of Mars between 1976 and 1980 by the two Viking landers and time-delay radar observations using the Mars Pathfinder lander made it possible to determine distances to Mars with an accuracy of about 10 metres (32 feet). The three largest asteroids—Ceres, Vesta, and Pallas—were found to cause departures of Mars from its predicted orbit in excess of 50 metres (164 feet) over times of 10 years or less. The measured departures, in turn, were used to estimate the masses of the three asteroids.

Masses for a number of other asteroids have been determined by noting their effect on the orbits of other asteroids that they approach closely and regularly, on the orbits of the asteroids' satellites, or on spacecraft orbiting or flying by the asteroids. For those asteroids whose diameters are determined and whose shapes are either spherical or ellipsoidal, their volumes are easily calculated. Knowledge of the mass and volume allows the density to be calculated. For asteroids with satellites, the density can be determined directly from the satellite's orbit without knowledge of the mass.

The orbital characteristics of NEAs mean that some of these objects make close approaches to Earth and occasionally collide with it. In January 1991, for example, an Apollo asteroid (or, as an alternative description, a large meteoroid) with an estimated diameter of 10 metres (33 feet) passed by Earth within less than half the distance to the Moon. Such passages are not especially unusual. On October 6, 2008, the asteroid 2008 TC3, which had a size of about 5 metres (16 feet), was discovered and crashed in the Nubian desert of the Sudan the next day. The collision of a sufficiently large NEA with Earth is generally recognized to pose a great potential danger to human beings and possibly to all life on the planet.

Because of the small sizes of NEAs and the short time they spend close enough to Earth to be seen, it is unusual for such close passages to be observed. An example of a NEA for which the lead time for observation is large is (99942) Apophis. This Aten asteroid, which has a diameter of about 300 m (984 feet), is predicted to pass within 32,000 km (19,884 miles) of Earth—i.e., closer than communications satellites in geostationary orbits—on April 13, 2029. During that passage, the probability of the asteroid hitting Earth is thought to be near zero. In 2006, however, it had been estimated that Apophis would have about 1 chance in 50,000 of colliding with Earth during the following close approach, on April 13, 2036.

ASTEROIDS, COMETS, AND THEIR DIFFERENCES

Asteroids traditionally have been distinguished from comets by characteristics based on physical differences, location in the solar system, and orbital properties. An object is classified as a comet when it displays "cometary activity"—i.e., a coma, or tail, or any evidence of gas or dust coming from it. In addition, any object on a nonreturning orbit (a parabolic or hyperbolic orbit, rather than an elliptical one) is generally considered to be a comet.

Although these distinctions apply most of the time, they are not always sufficient to classify an individual object as an asteroid or a comet. For example, an object found to be receding from the Sun on a nonreturning orbit and displaying no cometary activity could be a comet, or it could be a planet-crossing asteroid being ejected from the solar system after a close encounter with a planet, most likely

Jupiter. Unless such an object reveals itself by displaying cometary activity, there is usually no way to determine its origin and thus to classify it unequivocally. The object may have formed as an icy body, as comets do, but lost its volatile materials during a series of passes into the inner solar system. Its burned-out remnant of rocky material would presently have more physical characteristics in common with asteroids than with other comets.

CLASSIFYING ASTEROIDS

In the mid-1970s astronomers, using information gathered from studies of colour, spectral reflectance, and albedo, the fraction of incident radiation that is reflected by a surface or body, recognized that asteroids could be grouped into three broad taxonomic classes, designated C, S, and M. At that time they estimated that about 75 percent belonged to class C, 15 percent to class S, and 5 percent to class M. The remaining 5 percent were unclassifiable owing to either poor data or genuinely unusual properties. Furthermore, they noted that the S class dominated the population at the inner edge of the asteroid belt, whereas the C class was dominant in the middle and outer regions of the belt.

Within a decade this taxonomic system was expanded, and it was recognized that the asteroid belt comprised overlapping rings of differing taxonomic classes, with classes designated S, C, P, and D dominating the populations at distances from the Sun of about 2, 3, 4, and 5 AU, respectively. As more data became available from further observations, additional minor classes were recognized.

ASTEROID ROTATION AND SHAPE

The rotation periods and shapes of asteroids are determined primarily by monitoring their changing brightness on timescales of minutes to days. Short-period fluctuations in brightness caused by the rotation of an irregularly shaped asteroid or a spherical spotted asteroid (i.e., one with albedo differences) produce a light curve—a graph of brightness versus time—that repeats at regular intervals corresponding to an asteroid's rotation period. The range of brightness variation is closely related to an asteroid's shape or spottedness but is more difficult to interpret.

In the early years of the 21st century, rotation periods were known for more than 2,300 asteroids. They range from 42.7 seconds to 50 days, but more than 70 percent lie between 4 and 24 hours. In some cases, periods longer than a few days may actually be due to precession (a smooth slow circling of the rotation axis) caused by an unseen satellite of the asteroid. Periods on the order of minutes are observed only for very small objects (those with diameters less than about 150 metres [492 feet]). The largest asteroids (those with diameters greater than about 200 km [1,214 miles]) have a mean rotation period close to 8 hours; the value increases to 13 hours for asteroids with diameters of about 100 km (62 miles) and then decreases to about 6 hours for those with diameters of about 10 km (6 miles).

The largest asteroids may have preserved the rotation rates they had when they were formed, but the smaller ones almost certainly have had theirs modified by subsequent collisions and, in the case of the very smallest, perhaps also by radiation effects.

EXPLORING ASTEROIDS

The first mission to rendezvous with an asteroid was the Near Earth Asteroid Rendezvous (NEAR) spacecraft (later renamed NEAR Shoemaker), launched in 1996. The spacecraft entered orbit around (433) Eros, an S-class Amor asteroid, on February 14, 2000, where it spent a year

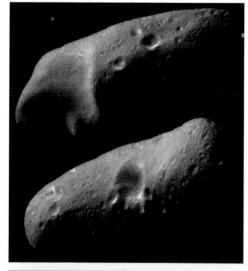

Opposite hemispheres of the asteroid Eros, shown in a pair of mosaics made from images taken by the U.S. Near Earth Asteroid Rendezvous (NEAR) Shoemaker spacecraft.

collecting images and other data before touching down on Eros's surface. Prior to this, spacecraft on the way to their primary targets, or as part of their overall mission, made close flybys of several asteroids. Although the time spent close enough to these asteroids to resolve them was a fraction of the asteroids' rotation periods, it was sufficient to image the portion of the surface illuminated at the time of the flyby and, in some cases, to obtain mass estimates.

The first asteroid studied during a close flyby was (951) Gaspra, which was observed in October 1991 by the Galileo spacecraft en route to Jupiter. Galileo's images, taken from a distance of about 5,000 km (3,107 miles), established that Gaspra, an S-class asteroid, is an irregular body with dimensions of 19 × 12 × 11 km (12 × 7 × 6.8 miles). Pocked with numerous small craters, Gaspra has an irregular shape and groovelike linear markings that suggest it was once part of a larger body that experienced one or more shattering collisions.

Photo montage showing Gaspra *(top)* compared with Deimos *(lower left)* and Phobos *(lower right)*, the moons of Mars.

Nearly two years later, in August 1993, Galileo flew by (243) Ida, another S-class asteroid. Ida was found to be somewhat crescent-shaped when viewed from the poles, with overall dimensions of about 56 × 15 km (35 × 9 miles), and to have a mean density of about 2.6 g/cm³ (1.5 oz/in³). After Galileo had passed Ida, examination of the images it took revealed a tiny object in orbit about the asteroid. Indirect evidence from as early as the 1970s had suggested the existence of natural satellites of asteroids, but Galileo provided the first confirmed instance of one. The moon was given the name Dactyl, from the Dactyli, a group of beings in Greek mythology who lived on Mount Ida in Crete.

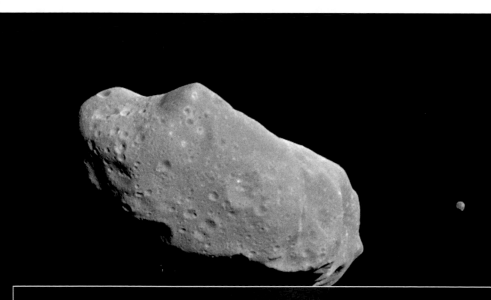

Asteroid Ida and its satellite, Dactyl, photographed by the Galileo spacecraft on August 28, 1993, from a distance of about 10,870 km (6,750 miles).

In 1999 astronomers using an Earth-based telescope equipped with adaptive optics discovered that the asteroid (45) Eugenia likewise has a moon. Once the orbit of an asteroid's moon has been established, it can be used to derive the density of the parent asteroid without knowing its mass. When this was done for Eugenia, its density turned out to be only 1.2 g/cm^3 (0.7 oz/in.^{3}). This implies that Eugenia has large voids in its interior, because the materials of which it is composed have densities greater than 2.5.

On its way to Eros, NEAR Shoemaker paid a brief visit to asteroid (253) Mathilde in June 1997. With a mean diameter of 56 km (35 miles), Mathilde is a main-belt asteroid and was the first C-class asteroid to be imaged. The object has a density similar to Eugenia's and likewise is thought to have a porous interior. In July 1999 the Deep Space 1 spacecraft flew by (9969) Braille at a distance of only 26 km (16 miles) during a mission to test a number of advanced technologies in deep space, and about a half year later, in January 2000, the Saturn-bound Cassini-Huygens spacecraft imaged asteroid (2685) Masursky from a comparatively far distance of 1.6 million km (994,194 miles). The Stardust spacecraft, on its way to collect dust from Comet Wild 2, flew by the main-belt asteroid (5535) Annefrank in November 2002, imaging the irregular object and determining it to be at least 6.6 km (4 miles) long, which is larger than estimated from Earth-based observations. The

Hayabusa spacecraft, designed to collect asteroidal material and return it to Earth, rendezvoused with the Apollo asteroid (25143) Itokawa between September and December 2005. It found the asteroid's dimensions to be 535 × 294 × 209 metres (1,755 × 965 × 685 feet) and its density to be 1.9 g/cm^3 (1.1 oz/in.^{3}).

The European Space Agency probe Rosetta on its way to Comet 67P/Churyumov-Gerasimenko flew by (2867) Steins on September 5, 2008, at a distance of 800 km (500 miles). Steins was the first E-class asteroid to be visited by a spacecraft and had a chain of seven craters on its surface. On August 6, 2014, it arrived at 67P/Churyumov-Gerasimenko. It became the first spacecraft to orbit a comet. On November 12, 2014, it's lander module, Philae, was the first to successfully touch down on a comet.

The most ambitious mission to the asteroid belt is that of the U.S. spacecraft Dawn, which was launched on September 27, 2007. Dawn arrived at Vesta on July 16, 2011, and Ceres on March 6, 2015.

THE ORIGIN OF ASTEROIDS

Available evidence indicates that the asteroids are the remnants of a "stillborn" planet. It is thought that at the time the planets were forming from the low-velocity collisions among asteroid-size planetesimals, one of them, Jupiter, grew at a high rate and to a size larger than the others. In the final stages of its formation, Jupiter gravitationally scattered large planetesimals, some of which may have been as massive as Earth is today. These planetesimals were eventually either captured by Jupiter or another of the giant planets or ejected from the solar system. While they were passing through the inner solar system, however, such large planetesimals strongly perturbed the orbits of the planetesimals in the region of the asteroid belt, raising their mutual velocities to the average 5 km (3 miles) per second they exhibit today. The increased velocities ended the accretionary collisions in this region by transforming them into catastrophic disruptions. Only objects larger than about 500 km (310 miles) in diameter could have survived collisions with objects of comparable size at collision velocities of 5 km (3 miles) per second. Since that time, the asteroids have been collisionally evolving so that, with the exception of the very largest, most present-day asteroids are either remnants or fragments of past collisions.

As collisions break down larger asteroids into smaller ones, they expose deeper layers of asteroidal material. If asteroids were compositionally homogeneous, this would have no noticeable result. Some of them, however, have become differentiated since their formation. This means that some asteroids, originally formed from so-called primitive material (i.e., material of solar composition with the volatile components removed), were heated, perhaps by short-lived radionuclides or solar magnetic induction, to the point where their interiors melted and geochemical processes occurred. In certain cases, temperatures became high enough for metallic iron to separate out. Being denser than other materials, the iron

The impact of a near-Earth object 66 million years ago in what is today the Caribbean region, as depicted in an artist's conception.

then sank to the centre, forming an iron core and forcing the less-dense basaltic lavas onto the surface. At least two asteroids with basaltic surfaces, Vesta and Magnya, survive to this day. Other differentiated asteroids, found today among the M-class asteroids, were disrupted by collisions that stripped away their crusts and mantles and exposed their iron cores. Still others may have had only their crusts partially stripped away, which exposed surfaces such as those visible today on the A-, E-, and R-class asteroids. Collisions were responsible for the formation of the Hirayama families and at least some of the planet-crossing asteroids.

CHAPTER 2

SHOOTING STARS: THE SCIENCE OF METEORS

A flaming streak flashes across the night sky and disappears. On rare occasions the flash of light plunges toward Earth, producing a boom like the thundering of guns and causing a great explosion when it lands. When ancient peoples witnessed such displays they believed they were seeing a star fall from the sky, so they called the object a shooting star or a falling star.

In modern usage the term "meteoroid," rather than being restricted to objects entering Earth's atmosphere, is applied to any small object in orbit around the Sun having the same nature as those that result in meteors. When a meteoroid enters Earth's atmosphere, it is traveling at very high velocity—more than 11 km per second (25,000 miles per hour) at minimum, which is many times faster than a bullet leaving a gun barrel. Frictional heating, produced by a meteoroid's energetic collision with atmospheric atoms and molecules, causes its surface to melt and vaporize and heats the air around it. The result is the luminous phenomenon recognized as a meteor.

Iron meteorite.

The vast majority of meteoroids that collide with Earth burn up in the upper atmosphere. If a meteoroid survives its fiery plunge through the atmosphere and lands on Earth's surface, the object is known as a meteorite.

The term "meteoroid" is usually reserved for chunks of matter that are approximately house-sized—i.e., some tens of metres across—and smaller, to distinguish them from the larger asteroidal bodies. Meteoroids are believed to be mostly fragments of asteroids and comets and are placed, with them, in the category of solar system objects known as small bodies. A few meteoroids also appear to have come from the Moon and Mars. The smallest meteoroids, those less than a few hundred micrometres across (about the size of a period on a printed page), are called interplanetary dust particles or micrometeoroids.

The terms "meteoroid" and "meteor" and "meteorite" are sometimes confusingly interchanged in common usage. Meteor in particular is often applied to a meteoroid hurtling through space, an incandescent meteoroid (rather than just its luminous streak) in the atmosphere, or an object that has hit the ground or a man-made object. An example of the last is found in the name Meteor Crater, a well-known impact structure in Arizona, United States.

METEOR FEATURES

On any clear night beyond the bright lights of cities, one can see with the naked eye several meteors per hour. Meteors can last for a small fraction of a second up to several seconds. Quite often, as the glowing meteoroid streaks through the sky, it varies in brightness, appears to emit sparks or flares, and sometimes leaves a luminous train that lingers after its flight has ended.

Unusually luminous meteors are termed "fireballs" or "bolides" (the latter term is often applied to those meteoroids observed to explode in the sky). When meteor rates increase significantly above normal, the phenomenon

A cloud trail left behind by a meteoroid stretches across the sky near Chelyabinsk in Siberia, Russia, on February 15, 2013.

is called a meteor shower. Meteors that do not appear to belong to showers are called sporadic.

Meteors are the result of the high-velocity collision of meteoroids with Earth's atmosphere. A typical visible meteor is produced by an object the size of a grain of sand and may start at altitudes of 100 km (60 miles) or higher. Meteoroids smaller than about 500 micrometres (μm; 0.02 inch) across are too faint to be seen with the naked eye but are observable with binoculars and telescopes; they can also be detected by radar. Brighter meteors—ranging in brilliance from that of Venus to greater than that of the full moon—are less common but are not really unusual. These are produced by meteoroids with masses ranging from several grams up to about one ton (centimetre- to metre-sized objects, respectively).

As meteoroids are traveling in interplanetary space near Earth, their velocities relative to Earth's range from a few kilometres per second up to as high as 72 km (44 miles) per second. As they draw closer to the planet, they are accelerated to yet higher velocities by Earth's gravitational field. The minimum velocity with which a meteoroid can enter the atmosphere is equal to Earth's escape velocity of 11.2 km (7 miles) per second. Even at this velocity, the kinetic energy for a meteoroid of a given mass is about 15 times that produced by an equal mass of chemical explosives such as TNT. As the meteoroid is slowed down by friction with atmospheric gas molecules, this kinetic energy is converted into heat. Even at the very low atmospheric density present at an altitude of 100 km (62 miles), this heat is sufficient to vaporize and ionize the surface material of the meteoroid and also to dissociate and ionize the surrounding atmospheric gas. The excitation of atmospheric and meteoroidal atoms produces a luminous region, which travels with the meteoroid and greatly exceeds its dimensions. About 0.1–1 percent of the original kinetic energy of the meteoroid is transformed into visible light, with most of the remainder going to heat up the air and the meteoroid and pushing aside the air that the meteoroid encounters.

At deeper levels in the atmosphere, a shock wave may develop in the air ahead of the meteoroid. The shock wave interacts with the solid meteoroid and its vapour in a complex way, and it can travel all the way to the ground even when the meteoroid does not. The penetration of a meteoroid in the kilogram range to altitudes of about 40 km (25 miles) can produce sounds on the ground similar to sonic booms or thunder. The sounds can even be intense enough to shake the ground and be recorded by seismometers designed to monitor earthquakes.

This great release of energy quickly destroys most meteoroids, particularly those with relatively high velocities. This destruction is the result both of ablation (the loss of mass from the surface of the meteoroid by vaporization or as molten droplets) and of fragmentation caused by aerodynamic pressure that exceeds the crushing strength of the meteoroid. For these reasons, numerous meteors end their observed flight at altitudes above 80 km (49 miles), and penetration to altitudes as low as 50 km (31 miles) is unusual.

The fragmentation of larger meteoroids due to the stresses of atmospheric entry is often catastrophic. About 10 large explosions (each equivalent to at least 1 kiloton of TNT, but some much larger) occur in the atmosphere every year. Explosions of this size are typically produced by meteoroids that are initially at least 2 metres (6 feet) across. For comparison, the atomic bomb dropped on Hiroshima, Japan, in 1945 had an explosive yield of 15 kilotons of TNT. A particularly spectacular explosion occurred over the Tunguska region of Siberia in Russia on June 30, 1908. The shock wave from that explosion, estimated to be equivalent to 15 megatons of TNT, flattened trees over an area almost 50 km across (about 2,000 square km [500,000 acres]). Witnesses reported that its brightness rivaled that of the Sun.

Despite the fiery end in store for most meteoroids, some lose their kinetic energy before they are completely destroyed. This can occur if the meteoroid is small and has a relatively low entry velocity (less than 25 km [15 miles] per second) or enters the atmosphere at a relatively shallow angle. It also can occur if the meteoroid has a large initial mass (greater than 100 grams [0.2 pound]) and fairly high crushing strength. Very small meteoroids—interplanetary dust particles less than 50–100 µm (0.002–0.004 inch)—are effectively stopped at considerable heights and may take weeks or months to settle out of the atmosphere. Because comet-derived particles tend to enter the atmosphere at high velocities, only those in the above-mentioned size range survive. Meteoroids as large as a few millimetres across that do survive melt either partially or completely and then resolidify.

Somewhat larger meteoroids—those as large as some tens of metres across— that reach the ground as meteorites melt at their surfaces while their interiors remain unheated. Even objects this large are effectively stopped by the atmosphere at altitudes of 5–25 km (3–15 miles), although they generally separate into fragments. Following this atmospheric braking, they begin to cool, their luminosity fades, and they fall to Earth at low velocities—100–200 metres per second (225–450 miles per hour). This "dark flight" may last several minutes, in contrast to the few seconds of visible flight as a meteor. By the time a meteoroid hits the ground, it has lost so much heat that the meteorite can be touched immediately with the bare hand. Often the only obvious sign on a meteorite of its fiery passage through the atmosphere is a dark, glassy crust, called a fusion crust, which is produced by melting of its surface. Sometimes meteorites also end up with aerodynamic shapes and flow structures on their surfaces. These features indicate that the meteoroid remained in the same orientation during atmospheric entry, much like manned spacecraft, rather than having tumbled as most meteoroids seem to do.

METEOR SHOWERS

Showers of meteors, in which the rate of meteor sightings temporarily increases at approximately the same time each year, have been recorded since ancient times. On rare occasions, such showers are very dramatic, with thousands of meteoroids falling per hour. More often, the usual hourly rate of roughly 5 observed meteors increases to about 10–50.

Meteors in showers characteristically are all moving in the same direction in space. As a consequence, plots of observed meteoroid trajectories on a map of the sky converge at a single point, the radiant of the shower, for the same reason that parallel railroad tracks appear to converge at a distance. A shower is usually named for the constellation (or for a star in the constellation) that contains its radiant. The introduction of photography to meteorite studies confirmed the theory developed from naked-eye observations that meteors belonging to a particular shower have not only the same radiant but simi-

Intense meteor outburst (yellow streaks) during the Perseid meteor shower of August 1995.

lar orbits as well. In other words, the meteoroids responsible for meteor showers move in confined streams (called meteor streams) around the Sun. The introduction of radar observation led to the discovery of new meteor showers—and thus of new meteor streams—that were invisible to the eye and to cameras because they came from radiants in the daytime sky. All told, about 2,000 showers have been identified.

Of great importance, and also fully confirmed by photographic data, is the association of several meteor showers with the orbits of active comets. As a comet travels near the Sun, it is heated and its abundant volatile ices (frozen gases) vaporize, releasing less volatile material in the form of dust and larger grains up to perhaps 1 cm (0.4 inch) across. The shower associated with a given comet thus represents debris shed from that comet along its orbit, which the orbit of Earth intersects annually. When Earth passes through this stream of debris, a meteor shower is produced.

The Leonid meteor shower represents a recently formed meteor stream. Though it occurs every year, this shower tends to increase greatly in visual strength every 33 or 34 years, which is the orbital period of the parent comet, Tempel-Tuttle. Such behaviour results from the fact that these meteoroids are mostly still clustered in a compact swarm moving in the orbit of the comet. Over

Observations of the Leonid meteor shower, 1870, made by the French aeronauts Henri Giffard and Wilfrid de Fonvielle during a trip in a hot-air balloon.

the next 1,000 years or so, the slightly different orbits of the meteoroids will disperse them more uniformly along the orbit of the comet. Meteor streams for which this has occurred produce showers that are usually weaker but often more consistent in strength from one occurrence to the next. Over a still longer period of about 10,000 years, gravitational perturbations by the planets will disperse the orbits of the meteoroids to the extent that their identities as members of a stream will disappear.

One strange example exists of a major meteor shower clearly associated with an object that at first glance does not resemble a comet. The parent object of the Geminid shower has all the appearances of a small Earth-crossing asteroid. Discovered in 1983, it does not exhibit the usual cometary features of a nebulous head and long tail and so was placed among the asteroids and named Phaethon. Most researchers believe Phaethon is the burned-out remnant of a once-active comet, but its nature may only be established with observations by spacecraft.

ENTERING EARTH'S ATMOSPHERE

The final impact of meteoroids about a kilogram (2.2 pounds) or less in mass with the ground is usually an anticlimax. The fall can go unnoticed even by those near the impact site, the impact being signaled only by a whistling sound and a thud. Many meteorites are recovered only because at least one fragment of the meteoroid strikes a house, car, or other object that draws the attention of local people to an unusual event. Recovered meteorites range in mass from a gram up to nearly 60 tons. Most meteorites consist either of stony—chiefly silicate—material (stony meteorites) or of primarily nickel-iron alloy (iron meteorites). In a small percentage of meteorites, nickel-iron alloy and silicate material are intermixed in approximately equal proportions (stony iron meteorites).

In addition to these relatively large meteorites, much smaller objects (less than a few millimetres across) can be recovered on Earth. The smallest, which are in the category of interplanetary dust particles and range from 10 to 100 μm (0.0004 to 0.004 inch) in diameter, are generally collected on filters attached to aircraft flying in the stratosphere at altitudes of at least 20 km (12 miles), where the concentration of terrestrial dust is low. On Earth's surface, somewhat larger micrometeorites have been collected from locations where other sources of dust are few and weathering rates are slow. These include sediments cored from the deep ocean, melt pools in the Greenland ice cap, and Antarctic ice that has been melted and filtered in large amounts. Researchers also have collected meteoroidal particles outside Earth's atmosphere with special apparatus on orbiting spacecraft, and in 2006 the Stardust mission returned dust that it had trapped in the vicinity of Comet Wild 2.

When meteoroids are sufficiently large—i.e., 100 metres (328 feet) to several kilometres in diameter—

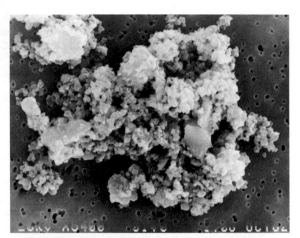

Interplanetary dust particle collected in Earth's atmosphere by a NASA high-altitude research aircraft and imaged in an electron microscope.

they pass through the atmosphere without slowing down appreciably. As a result, they strike Earth's surface at velocities of many kilometres per second. The huge amount of kinetic energy released in such a violent collision is sufficient to produce an impact crater. In many ways, impact craters resemble those produced by nuclear explosions. They are often called meteorite craters, even though almost all of the impacting meteoroids themselves are vaporized during the explosion.

The geologic record of cratering on Earth (and many other bodies in the solar system) attests to the power of the impact of meteoroids, including objects with kinetic energies equivalent to as much as one billion megatons of TNT. Fortunately, impacts of this magnitude now occur only once or twice every 100 million years, but they were much more common in the first 500 million years of solar system history. At that time, as planet formation was winding down, the asteroid-size planetesimals that were left over were being swept up by the new planets. The intensity of the bombardment during this period, often referred to as the late heavy bombardment, can be seen in the ancient, heavily cratered terrains of the Moon, Mars, Mercury, and many other bodies.

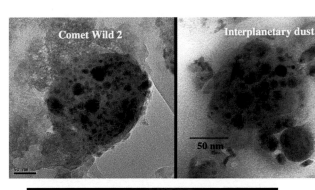

Microscopic components of dust particles collected from the vicinity of Comet Wild 2 *(left)* and interplanetary space *(right)* by the Stardust mission and returned to Earth.

Some scientists have suggested that very large impacts may have played a major role in determining the origin of life on Earth and the course of biological evolution. The first signs of life are found in rocks that are only slightly younger than the end of the late heavy bombardment. Until the end of the bombardment, life could have started many times but would have been repeatedly wiped out by large impacts that boiled the oceans and melted the surface rocks. When life did finally establish a foothold, it may have done so in the deep

METEOR CRATER

Arizona's Meteor Crater is a rimmed, bowl-shaped pit produced by a large meteorite in the rolling plain of the Canyon Diablo region, 30 km (19 miles) west of Winslow, Arizona. It is one of the best-preserved terrestrial impact craters.

The crater is 1,200 metres (4,000 feet) in diameter and about 180 metres (600 feet) deep inside

Meteor Crater was excavated by the explosive impact of an object with a diameter of perhaps 50 metres (160 feet).

its rim, which rises nearly 60 metres (200 feet) above the plain. Drillings reveal undisturbed rock beneath 213–244 metres (700–800 feet) of fill. The strata forming the rim of the crater are upturned and covered with the debris of the same bedrock, which shows an inverted stratigraphy.

Discovered in 1891, its age has been variously estimated at between 5,000 and 50,000 years. Large numbers of nickel-iron fragments from gravel size to

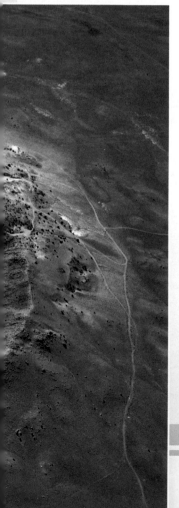

640 kg (1,400 pounds) have been found in a 260 square km (100 square mile) area. The distribution and composition of several thousand tons of sand-grain size nickel–iron droplets indicate that they condensed from a cloud of metallic vapours. Surveys show only fragments within the pit, but the 1960 discovery there of coesite and stishovite, which are high-pressure modifications of silica, helped to confirm the crater's meteoritic origin, a position that had been argued for 27 years by Philadelphia mining engineer D.M. Barringer.

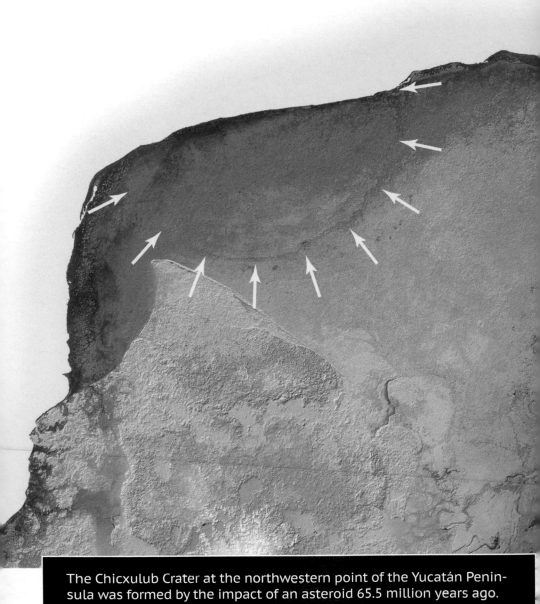

The Chicxulub Crater at the northwestern point of the Yucatán Peninsula was formed by the impact of an asteroid 65.5 million years ago.

oceans or deep in Earth's crust where it would have been protected from all but the largest impacts. Later, once impact rates had dropped dramatically and life was well-established, rare large impacts may have altered the course of evolution by causing simultaneous extinctions of many species.

Perhaps the best-known of these associations is the mass extinction believed by many scientists to have been triggered by a huge impact some 65 million years ago, near the end of the Cretaceous Period. The most-cited victims of this impact were the dinosaurs, whose demise led to the replacement of reptiles by mammals as the dominant land animals and eventually to the rise of the human species. The object responsible for this

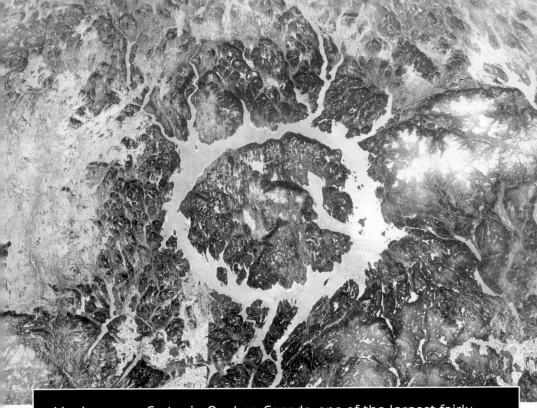

Manicouagan Crater in Quebec, Canada, one of the largest fairly well-preserved impact craters on Earth, as seen from the International Space Station on April 28, 2002.

destruction is estimated to have been about 10 km (6 miles) across, and it produced a crater roughly 150 km (93 miles) in diameter that is thought to be buried under sediments of the Yucatán Peninsula in Mexico.

CHAPTER 3

STUDYING METEORITES

Almost all meteoroids are formed from material that breaks off comets or asteroids. If a meteoroid survives its fall and reaches Earth's surface, it is called a meteorite. In modern usage the term "meteorite" is broadly applied to similar objects that land on the surface of other comparatively large bodies. For instance, meteorite fragments have been found in samples returned from the Moon, and at least 10 meteorites have been identified on the surface of Mars by robotic rovers. The largest meteorite that has been identified on Earth was found in 1920 in Namibia. Named the Hoba meteorite, it measures 2.7 metres (9 feet) across, is estimated to weigh nearly 60 tons, and is made of an alloy of iron and nickel. The smallest meteorites, called micrometeorites, range in size from a few hundred micrometres (μm) to as small as about 10 μm (0.0004 inch) and come from the population of tiny particles that fill interplanetary space.

The principal driving force behind meteorite studies is the fact that small bodies such as asteroids and comets are most likely to preserve evidence of events that took place in the early solar system. There are at least two reasons to expect that this is the case. First, when the solar system began to form, it was composed of gas and fine-grained dust. The assembly of planet-size bodies from this dust almost certainly involved the coming together of smaller objects to make successively larger ones, beginning with

Hoba meteorite, lying where it was discovered in 1920, in Grootfontein, Namibia.

dust balls and ending, in the inner solar system, with the rocky, or terrestrial, planets—Mercury, Venus, Earth, and Mars. In the outer solar system the formation of Jupiter, Saturn, and the other giant planets is thought to have involved more than simple aggregation, but their moons—and comets—probably did form by this basic mechanism. Available evidence indicates that asteroids and comets are leftovers of the intermediate stages of the aggregation mechanism. They are therefore representative of bodies

that formed quite early in the history of the solar system.

Second, in the early solar system various processes were in operation that heated up solid bodies. The primary ones were decay of short-lived radioactive isotopes within the bodies and collisions between the bodies as they grew. As a result, the interiors of larger bodies experienced substantial melting, with consequent physical and chemical changes to their constituents. Smaller bodies, on the other hand, generally radiated away this heat quite efficiently, which allowed their interiors to remain relatively cool. Consequently, they should preserve to some

Scientists of the Antarctic Search for Meteorites (ANSMET) team log and collect a meteorite discovered lying on an ice field.

degree the dust and other material from which they formed. Indeed, certain meteorites do appear to preserve very ancient material, some of which predates the solar system.

Meteorites traditionally are given the name of a geographic feature associated with the location where they are found. Until quite recently, there were no systematic efforts to recover them. This was largely because meteorites fall more or less uniformly over Earth's surface and because there was no obvious way to predict where they would fall or could be found. When a meteorite was seen to fall or when a person chanced upon an unusual-looking rock, the specimen was simply taken to a museum or a private collector.

THE DIFFERENT TYPES OF METEORITES

Meteorites traditionally have been divided into three broad categories—stony meteorites (or stones), iron meteorites (irons), and stony iron meteorites (stony irons)— based on the proportions of rock-forming minerals and nickel-iron (also called iron-nickel) metal alloy they contain. Stony meteorites make up about 94 percent of all known meteorites, irons about 5 percent, and stony irons about 1 percent. There is considerable diversity within each category, leading to numerous subdivisions (classes, groups, etc.) based on variations in chemistry, mineralogy, and structure.

It is important to realize that meteorite classification is based primarily on observable characteristics. Just because subdivisions belong to the same category, it does not necessarily follow that they all consist of meteorites that have the same or similar parent bodies. Indeed, more often than not, they are unrelated. Conversely, subdivisions from different categories may have a common origin. For instance, if a large asteroid were to melt, its denser metallic components would tend to sink to its centre (its core), while its less-dense rocky material would form a mantle around it, much like what happened to Earth. This separation process is known as geochemical differentiation. When the differentiated asteroid is later broken up by collisions, samples of its rocky mantle, iron core, and core-mantle interface

Small samples of iron meteorites.

might be represented in the three main categories. Thus, the challenge for researchers is to determine which types of meteorites are related and which are not, as well as to identify the processes that were responsible for the tremendous diversity that is seen among them.

CHONDRITES

The most fundamental distinction between the various stony meteorites is between those that were once molten, the achondrites, and those that were not, the chondrites. Chondrites have been subdivided into three main classes—ordinary, carbonaceous, and enstatite chondrites—and these in turn have been divided into a number of groups.

Orgueil, a chondrite that fell in southwestern France in 1864.

Chondrites are the most abundant meteorites (about 87 percent of stony meteorites) in collections. They also are arguably the most important. In terms of terrestrial rocks, these meteorites seem akin to sedimentary conglomerates—i.e., fragments of preexisting rock cemented together. They are a mechanical mixture of components that formed in the solar nebula or even earlier. Perhaps more remarkably, the compositions of chondrites are very similar to that of the Sun, except for the absence (in chondrites) of very volatile elements such as hydrogen and helium. The Sun contains more than 99 percent of the mass of the solar system. The composition of the Sun must therefore be very close to the average composition of the solar system when it formed. As a result, the Sun's composition can serve as a reference. Deviations in a meteorite's composition from this reference composition provide clues to the processes that influenced the formation of its parent body and the components in it.

CHONDRULES

Meteorites are classified as chondrites based on the presence within them of small spherical bodies (typically about 1 mm [0.04 inch] in diameter) called chondrules. From their shapes and the texture of the crystals in them, chondrules appear to have been free-floating molten droplets in the solar nebula. Simulation experiments show that chondrules formed by "ash" heating (to peak temperatures of 1,400–1,800 °C) and then rapid cooling (10–1,000 °C per hour).

The sizes, compositions, and proportions of different types of chondrules vary from one chondrite meteorite to the next, which means that chondrule formation must have been a fairly localized process. There is also good evidence for its occurring many times. If chondrule abundance in chondrites is any guide, the chondrule-forming process was one of the most energetic and important in the solar nebula, at least in the region of the asteroid belt. Nevertheless, despite more than a century of study and speculation, scientists have yet to determine definitively what the process was.

METEORITICS: THE SCIENCE OF METEORS AND METEORITES

The scientific discipline concerned with meteors and meteorites is called meteoritics. The awe-inspiring noise and lights accompanying some meteoric falls convinced early humans that meteorites came from the gods; accordingly these objects were widely regarded with awe and veneration. This association of meteorites with the miraculous and religious made 18th-century scientists suspicious of their reality. Members of the French Academy, which was then considered the highest scientific authority, were convinced that the fall of stones from heaven was impossible. Keepers of European museums discarded genuine meteorites as shameful relics of a superstitious past. Against this background, the German physicist Ernst Florens Friedrich Chladni began the science of meteoritics in 1794, when he defended the trustworthiness of accounts of falls. A shower of stones that fell in 1803 at L'Aigle, France, finally convinced the scientific world of the reality of meteorites. Interest was intensified by the great meteor shower of November 12, 1833, which was visible in North America. Most natural-history museums now have meteorite collections.

For many years the only method of observing meteors was with the naked eye. The observer would plot the path of a meteor among the stars on a chart and note its apparent magnitude, the time, and other information. A similar plot of the same meteor made about 60 km (40 miles) away permitted rough estimates to be made of its altitude and the true angle of its path. This data can now be obtained more accurately with photographic or radar techniques, but visual observation continues to provide information on the magnitudes of meteors and serves as a check of instrumental methods.

ACHONDRITES

Achondrites, their name meaning "without chondrites," are a relatively small but diverse group of meteorites. They exhibit a range of features that would be expected if their parent bodies experienced wide-spread melting: igneous features similar to those observed in terrestrial volcanic rocks, segregation of molten metal (possibly into a core) from molten silicate rock (magma), and magmatic segregation of silicate crystals and melt. Most achondrites collected on Earth are derived from asteroids, but one small group is thought to come from Mars and another from the Moon.

Hypersthene crystals are embedded in this brecciated diogenite achondrite.

The three most numerous asteroidal achondrite groups are the aubrites, the howardite-eucrite-diogenite association, and the ureilites. Aubrites are also known as enstatite achondrites. Like the enstatite class of chondrites, the aubrites derive from parent bodies that formed under highly chemically reducing conditions. As a result, they contain elements in the form of less-common compounds—for example, calcium as the sulfide mineral oldhamite (CaS) rather than in its more usual silicate and carbonate forms.

The howardite, eucrite, and diogenite (HED) meteorites all seem to be related to one another and probably came from the same asteroidal body, tentatively identified as Vesta, the second largest member of the asteroid belt. They have also been linked to the mesosiderites, a group of stony iron meteorites. The HED parent body seems to have had a complex history that included melting, segregation of metal into a core, crystallization, metamorphism, and impact brecciation (the process in which an impact shatters rock).

The eucrites are subdivided into cumulate eucrites and basaltic eucrites. Cumulate eucrites are like terrestrial gabbros in that they seem to have formed at depth in their parent body and crystallized quite slowly. By contrast, basaltic eucrites are similar to terrestrial basalts, apparently having formed at or near the surface of their parent body and cooled relatively fast. The diogenites, composed predominantly of the mineral pyroxene, also seem to have formed at depth. The howardites are impact breccias composed of cemented fragments of diogenite and eucrite materials.

The third main class of asteroid-derived achondrites, the ureilites, are carbon-bearing. They consist of a silicate rock, made primarily of the minerals olivine and pyroxene, that has dark veins running through it. The veins, which constitute as much as 10 percent of the meteorites, are composed of carbon (graphite and some diamond), nickel-iron metal, and sulfides. The silicates clearly crystallized from magma, but there is debate about how they formed. The carbon-rich veins seem to have formed by shock-induced redistribution of graphite that originally crystallized along with the silicates. In addition to the three main achondrite classes, there exist several minor classes and a collection of unique achondrite specimens, all of which reflect the variability of melting processes in the asteroids.

More than 200 meteorites have been identified as having come from Mars, and all are volcanic rocks. All but one of these belong to one of three classes—shergottites, nakhlites, and chassignites—which were established well before a Martian origin was suspected. The three groups are often referred to collectively as SNCs. One piece of evidence for a planetary origin of the SNCs is their young age, between 150 million and 1.3 billion years. To retain enough heat so that volcanic activity could continue until just 1.3 billion years ago, let alone more recently, required a planet-sized parent body. Because there is considerable geochemical evidence that the rocks did not originate on Earth, the only likely candidates that remain are Venus and Mars, both of which appear to have experienced recent volcanic activity.

A number of lunar meteorites have been found in Antarctica and hot deserts on Earth. They probably would not have been recognized as having come from the Moon were it not for the lunar samples brought back by the manned Apollo and robotic Luna missions. The meteorites, which likely are fragments blasted off the Moon by large impacts, resemble the various rock types represented in the lunar samples (e.g., mare basalts, highland regolith breccias, and highland impact-melt breccias), but they almost certainly came from areas that were not sampled by the various missions. Therefore, like the Martian meteorites,

EETA79001, a meteorite classified as a shergottite that provides the best evidence, from analysis of its trapped gases, that some meteorites are from Mars.

they are an important source of new information on the formation and evolution of their parent body.

METEORITES COMPOSED OF IRON

Iron meteorites are pieces of denser metal that segregated from the less-dense silicates when their parent bodies were at least partially melted. They most probably came from the cores of their parent asteroids, although some researchers have suggested that metal, rather than forming a single repository, may have pooled more locally, producing a structure resembling raisin bread, with metal chunks as the "raisins." The latter would have been likely to occur if the asteroid underwent localized shock melting rather than melting of the entire body.

Iron meteorites are principally composed of two nickel-iron minerals, nickel-poor kamacite and nickel-rich taenite. The abundances of these two minerals strongly influence the structure of iron meteorites. At one extreme is the class known as hexahedrites, which are composed almost entirely of kamacite. Being nearly of a single mineral, hexahedrites are essentially structureless except for shock features. At the other extreme is the class known as ataxites, which are made up primarily of taenite. Ataxites are the rarest class and can contain up to about 60 percent nickel by weight. Again, because they are nearly monomineralic, they are almost featureless structurally. Between these two classes are the octahedrites. In these meteorites, kamacite crystals form as interlocking plates in an octahedral arrangement, with taenite filling the interstices. This interlocking arrangement, called the Widmanstätten pattern, is revealed when a cut and polished surface of the meteorite is etched with dilute acid. The pattern is an indication that octahedrites formed at relatively low pressure, as would be expected if they formed in asteroid-sized bodies.

ASSOCIATION OF METEORITES WITH ASTEROIDS

If meteoritic material comes from specific regions of the asteroid belt, then the asteroids in such regions should have the chemical and mineralogical composition observed in the meteorites. The surface mineralogical composition of asteroids, in principle, can be determined directly by observations from Earth of the albedo and the spectrum of the reflected light (reflectance spectrum). A number of

Widmanstätten pattern seen in a octahedrite.

processes conspire, however, to make the association of certain asteroids with the various meteorite groups much more difficult than might be expected.

Although no two asteroidal reflectance spectra are exactly alike in detail, most asteroids fall into one of two general groups, the S class and the C class. S class asteroids (e.g., Gaspra and Ida, observed by the Galileo spacecraft, and Eros, visited by the NEAR Shoemaker spacecraft) have moderate albedos and contain mixtures of olivine, pyroxene, and metallic iron. These are the same minerals found in ordinary chondrites, but they also are present in a number of other meteorite types. The C class asteroids (e.g., Mathilde, observed by NEAR Shoemaker) have low albedos, and their more featureless spectra indicate the presence of light-absorbing materials, although at least half have a spectral feature associated with iron-bearing hydrous silicates. It is plausible to consider the C class asteroids as candidate sources for certain groups of carbonaceous chondrite meteorites. Their low albedos and spectral evidence of hydrous silicates, however, make them unlikely sources of ordinary chondrites.

When the S class asteroids are considered in more detail, there are difficulties in identifying them all as sources of ordinary chondrites. Largely because of their apparent range of mineralogies—specifically their ratios of olivine to pyroxene—the S class asteroids have been

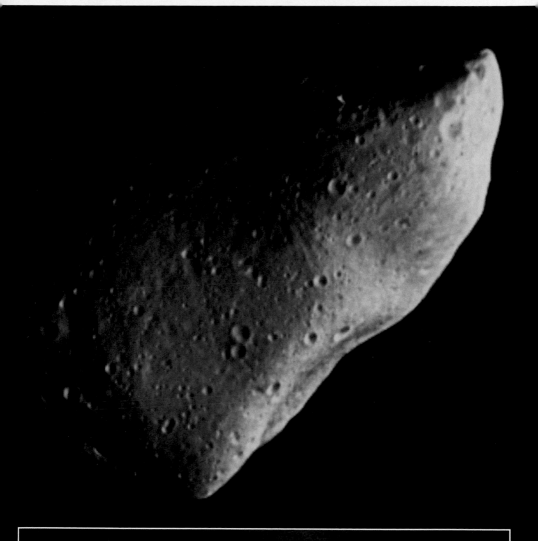

Asteroid 951 Gaspra, taken by Galileo spacecraft, October 29, 1991.

divided into seven subclasses. In light of this, it is possible that the S class actually represents a number of unrelated groups of asteroids. In addition, some research has linked the S class asteroids to several groups of achondrites. On the other hand, if most S type asteroids are not related to the ordinary chondrites, scientists would be challenged to explain how an uncommon and unidentified class of asteroid is supplying most of the meteorites to Earth.

The asteroids in the S(IV) subclass seem to have mineralogies that best match those of the ordinary chondrites. This is supported by measurements made by NEAR Shoemaker of the elemental composition of the surface of Eros, which is classified as an S(IV) asteroid. With the notable exception of a low sulfur content, the composition of Eros was found to be consistent with that of an ordinary chondrite.

Scientists have come to recognize relatively recently that the surfaces of asteroids and other solid bodies are not necessarily representative of what lies just a short distance beneath those surfaces. Both Eros's low-sulfur measurement and the fact that, overall, the spectra of S class asteroids do not exactly match those of ordinary chondrites may be due, at least partially, to the effects of a poorly understood set of processes collectively called space weathering. Important component processes of space weathering are thought to be the impacts of meteorites and micro-meteorites and the impingement of energetic solar wind particles and solar radiation on surface materials. Over time these processes act to modify the chemical and physical surface properties of airless bodies such as Mercury, the Moon and some other planetary satellites, and asteroids and comets.

Comparisons of younger surfaces around craters with older terrains on Eros by NEAR Shoemaker, and on Gaspra and Ida by Galileo, support the idea that space weathering occurs on asteroids.

Asteroids are thought to be covered by a layer of pulverized rock, called regolith, produced by bombardment with meteorites of all sizes over millions to billions of years. The regolith need only be as thin as a few sheets of paper to completely mask the underlying material from reflectance spectroscopy, although on most asteroids it is probably much thicker. Unfortunately, because it is so loosely bound together, this regolith material does not survive entry into Earth's atmosphere in pieces that are large enough to identify as meteorites and analyze. Consequently, scientists do not have samples of regolith that can be compared with meteorites or asteroids directly. On the Moon, however, systematic changes are observed in the mineralogy and reflectance properties of the surface material as a result of this collisional grinding and other space weathering processes. Thus, although it seems likely that ordinary chondrites do come from S class asteroids, space weathering may be making it di cult to determine with certainty which S class asteroids are the parent bodies of these meteorites and which are unrelated but have a grossly similar mineralogy.

METEORITE CRATERS

When a meteorite impacts with Earth or with other comparatively large solid bodies such as the Moon, other planets and their satellites, or larger asteroids and comets, a depression results that is called a meteorite crater. For this discussion, the term "meteorite crater" is considered to be synonymous with impact crater. As such, the colliding objects are not restricted by size to meteorites as they are found on Earth. Rather, they include chunks of solid material of the same nature as comets or asteroids and in a wide range of sizes—from small meteoroids up to comets and asteroids themselves.

Meteorite crater formation is arguably the most important geologic process in the solar system, as meteorite craters cover most solid-surface bodies, Earth being a notable exception. Meteorite craters can be found not only on rocky surfaces like that of the Moon but also on the surfaces of comets and ice-covered moons of the outer planets. Formation of the solar system left countless pieces of debris in the form of asteroids and comets and their fragments. Gravitational interactions with other objects routinely send this debris on a collision course with planets and their moons. The resulting impact from a piece of debris produces a surface depression many times larger than the original object.

Although all meteorite craters are grossly similar, their appearance varies substantially with both size and the body on which they occur. If no other geologic processes have occurred on a planet or moon, its entire surface is covered with craters as a result of the impacts sustained over the past 4.6 billion years since the major bodies of the solar system formed. On the other hand, the absence or sparseness of craters on a body's surface, as is the case for Earth's surface, is an indicator of some other geologic process (e.g., erosion or surface melting) occurring during the body's history that is eliminating the craters.

The heavily cratered far side of the Moon, photographed by Apollo 16 astronauts in April 1972.

Space weathering must also affect the spectra of the asteroidal sources of the other meteorite groups. Nevertheless, a number of more-or-less convincing associations between groups of meteorites and types of asteroids have been made. It has been proposed that the CV and CO groups of carbonaceous chondrites come from the K class asteroids. As mentioned above, a number of lines of evidence, including spectral measurements, point to the asteroid Vesta being the source of the howardite-eucrite-diogenite association and the mesosiderites. The most likely source of the iron meteorites is the M class of asteroids, but enstatite chondrites and mesosiderites have also been linked to them. The pallasites may come from A class asteroids.

METEORITES AND THE EARLY SOLAR SYSTEM

As mentioned, scientists study meteorites for insights into the events that took place surrounding the birth and early evolution of the solar system. They know from astronomical observations that all stars form by gravitational collapse of dense regions in interstellar molecular clouds. This is almost certainly how the solar nebula formed, and the presence of preserved circumstellar and interstellar material in meteorites is consistent with this idea. Less clear is what precipitated the gravitational collapse of the region of the molecular cloud that became the solar system.

Gravitational collapse can occur spontaneously—i.e., through random fluctuations of density. Another possibility, however, is suggested by the finding in meteorites (particularly in their refractory inclusions) of short-lived radionuclides that were present at formation (as opposed to the later production of radionuclides by recent cosmic-ray irradiation). The shortest-lived of the radionuclides found to date, calcium-41, has a half-life of only about 100,000 years. This radionuclide must have been made and incorporated into refractory inclusions within just a few half-lives (less than a million years), or its abundance would have been too low to detect. This is remarkably short by astronomical standards. Because the other short-lived radionuclides have longer half-lives, they do not put such stringent time constraints on the interval between their synthesis and formation of refractory inclusions. Nevertheless, the absolute and relative abundances of the short-lived radionuclides can be compared with the values predicted for likely sources of the radionuclides.

One potential source of radionuclides is nucleosynthesis in stars ending their lives in catastrophic explosions called supernovas and in a class of dying stars known as asymptotic giant branch (AGB) stars. Both supernovas and AGB stars produce massive, fast-moving winds (flows of matter) that are rich in short-lived radionuclides. Numerical simulations show that under some conditions, when these winds hit an interstellar molecular cloud that cannot collapse spontaneously, they compress it to the point that it becomes gravitationally unstable and collapses. The simulations also show that some of the wind material with its complement of short-lived radionuclides is mixed into the collapsing cloud. Thus, in this scenario, the radionuclides are fingerprints of the stellar wind responsible for triggering the collapse of the molecular cloud that evolved into the Sun and planets.

An alternative explanation for the short-lived radionuclides in meteorites has not been ruled out—their synthesis in the solar nebula by intense radiation from an early active Sun. This concept has proved somewhat less successful than the stellar-wind idea at explaining the absolute and relative abundances of the short-lived radionuclides. Nevertheless, no model incorporating either of these explanations has been completely successful in this regard.

After collapse was initiated, the first solids known to have formed in the solar nebula were the refractory inclusions, which apparently were made in relatively short-lived heating events about 4,567,000,000 years ago. The gradation of planetary compositions from dry, rocky, metal-rich Mercury to gas-rich Jupiter and its icy moons suggests that there was a temperature gradient in the inner solar system.

Astrophysical models predict such gradients, although the absolute value of the gradient varies with the conditions assumed for a given model. One of many ideas for producing the refractory inclusions is that they formed in convection currents circulating at the edge of the hottest region of the inner nebula.

The ambient environment in the asteroid belt at the time the asteroids were being assembled must have been thermally a rather tranquil one. The fact that presolar material is preserved in meteorites argues against widespread heating of the asteroidal region, as do the presence of water-bearing minerals and the relatively high content of volatile elements in many chondrites. Again, this is consistent with most current astrophysical models. Despite the evidence for an overall low temperature in this region of the solar system, the abundance of chondrules in all chondritic meteorites except the CI chondrites attest to local, transient episodes of very high temperatures.

If chondrules were relatively rare in meteorites, their formation could be regarded as of secondary importance in the early solar system. Chondrules and their fragments, however, make up most of the mass of the most abundant class of meteorites, the ordinary chondrites, and a major portion of other chondrites, which indicates that their formation must have been of central importance. Even if the parent bodies of ordinary chondrites formed only within a restricted region of the asteroid belt adjacent to the major resonance that is thought to put chondritic material into Earth-crossing orbits, this region still represents about 10 percent of the asteroid belt. It also is likely that the parent asteroids of other chondrule-bearing meteorites formed outside this region, even though they may be in that region today.

Ideas abound for how chondrules formed—e.g., electrical discharges, shock waves, collisions between molten asteroids, and outflows associated with the early active Sun—but none has gained general acceptance. The ages of chondrules are crucial to distinguishing between some of these ideas. If they really formed over a period of 1–10 million years after refractory inclusions, this would be problematic for certain models. Fewer problems would arise if it turned out that the measured ages of most chondrules reflect when they were reheated or altered in their parent body.

Asteroidal bodies began to form perhaps as early as one million years after refractory inclusions. Certainly, within 5–10 million years they were being heated, aqueously altered, and melted. Volcanic activity on some asteroidal bodies, presumably the larger ones, continued for as long as about 170 million years. The process responsible for this heating remains to be clearly identified. The short-lived radioactive isotopes aluminum-26 and iron-60 appear to be the most likely heat sources, but heat from electric currents induced by early solar activity and from the release of gravitational potential energy as asteroids formed also may have contributed.

Asteroid-sized bodies presumably were forming not just in the asteroid belt but everywhere in the solar system. Concurrently, they would have begun aggregating into larger bodies in a process that eventually produced the rocky inner planets. This process was remarkably rapid. The Moon probably formed by an impact of a Mars-sized body with the growing Earth. The oldest Moon rocks that have been dated are about 4.44 billion years old, but there is evidence that the Moon actually formed within 30 million years of the refractory inclusions. Similarly, the oldest meteoritic material from Mars is about 4.5 billion years old, but there is evidence that Mars itself formed about 13 million years after the refractory inclusions. Thus, within as little as 30 million years of the appearance of the first solids, the aggregation process that started with tiny particles had produced the rocky inner planets.

In order for asteroids to have formed and developed at all on the timescale of a few million years, theoretical calculations suggest that the density of matter required was more like that in the regions occupied by the giant planets. The quantity of material observed in the asteroid belt today, however, is quite small, perhaps as little as 1/10,000 of that originally present. Some natural process must have removed almost all the material in this region of the solar system after the formation of the asteroidal bodies.

Although the details are not yet fully understood, it seems most likely that the formation of the giant planets, particularly Jupiter, quickly resulted in the evacuation of most of the matter from this region of the solar system.

The foregoing scenario of early solar system evolution is likely to be wrong in some, and perhaps many, of the details. Nevertheless, without the samples of asteroids and primitive solar system materials provided by meteorites, there would be little observational basis at all for formulating models of this kind. For good reason, meteorites have been dubbed "poor man's space probes." Until spacecraft missions bring back a variety of samples from asteroids and comets, the most precise and detailed data for the evolution of the solar system will come from meteorites.

CHAPTER 4

THE UNIVERSE OF COMETS

A comet is a small chunk of dust and ice that orbits the Sun. When near the Sun, comets develop a hazy cloud of gases and dust. They also often develop long, glowing tails. However, a comet exists as only a small core of ice and dust for most or even its entire orbit around the Sun. It is sometimes described as a "dirty snowball."

Many comets do not develop tails; moreover, comets are not surrounded by nebulosity during most of their lifetime. The only permanent feature of a comet is its nucleus, which is a small body that may be seen as a stellar image in large telescopes when tail and nebulosity do not exist, particularly when the comet is still far away from the Sun.

Two characteristics differentiate the cometary nucleus from a very small asteroid—namely, its orbit and its chemical nature. A comet's orbit is more eccentric; therefore, its distance to the Sun varies considerably. Its material is more volatile. When far from the Sun, however, a comet remains in its pristine state for eons without losing any volatile

The multiple impact sites in the southern hemisphere of Jupiter by Comet Shoemaker-Levy 9.

components because of the deep cold of space. For this reason, astronomers believe that pristine cometary nuclei may represent the oldest and best-preserved material in the solar system.

During a close passage near the Sun, the nucleus of a comet loses water vapour and other more volatile compounds, as well as dust dragged away by the sublimating gases. It is then surrounded by a transient dusty "atmosphere" that is steadily lost to space. This feature is the coma, which gives a comet its nebulous appearance.

The nucleus surrounded by the coma makes up the head of the comet. When it is even closer to the Sun, solar radiation usually blows the dust of the coma away from the head and produces a dust tail, which is often rather wide, featureless, and yellowish. The solar wind, on the other hand, drags ionized gas away in a slightly different direction and produces a plasma tail, which is usually narrow with nods and twists and has a bluish appearance.

CLASSIFYING COMETS

In order to classify the chronological appearance of comets, the *Astronomische Nachrichten* ("Astronomical Reports") introduced in 1870 a system of preliminary and final designations that was used until 1995. The preliminary designation classified comets according to their order of discovery, using the year of discovery followed by a lowercase letter in alphabetical order, as in 1987a, 1987b, 1987c, and so forth. Comets were then reclassified as soon as possible— usually a few years later—according to their chronological order of passage at perihelion (closest distance to the Sun); a Roman numeral was used, as in 1987 I, 1987 II, 1987 III, and so on.

In 1995 the International Astronomical Union (IAU) simplified the designation of comets since the two chronologies of letters and Roman numerals were often the same, and redesignating a comet after its perihelion was confusing. A newly discovered comet is called by the year in which it was discovered, then by a letter corresponding to the half-month of discovery, and finally a number denoting its order in that half-month. For example, Comet Hale-Bopp was 1995 O1. The official designation generally includes the name(s) of its discoverer(s)—with a maximum of three names—preceded by a P/ if the comet is on a periodic orbit of less than 200 years. If a comet has been observed at two perihelions, it is given a permanent number. For example, Halley's Comet is 1P/Halley since it was the first comet determined to be periodic. Comets with longer periods or that will not return to the inner solar system are preceded by a C/.

The discoverer's rule has not always been strictly applied: comets 1P/Halley, 2P/Encke, and 27P/Crommelin have been named after the astronomers who proved their periodic character. In the past, some comets became bright so fast that they were discovered by a large number of persons at almost the same time. They are given an arbitrary impersonal designation such as the Great September Comet (C/1882 R1), Southern Comet (C/1947 X1), or Eclipse Comet (C/1948 V1). Finally, comets may be discovered by an unusual instrument without direct intervention of a specific observer, as in the case of the Earth-orbiting Infrared Astronomical Satellite (IRAS). Its initials are used as if it were a human observer, as in C/1983 H1 IRAS-Araki-Alcock.

EARLY STUDY OF COMETS

In ancient times, without interference from streetlights or urban pollution, comets could be seen by everyone. Their sudden appearance was interpreted as an omen of nature that awed people and was used by astrologers to predict flood, famine, pestilence, or the death of kings. The Greek philosopher Aristotle (4th century BCE) thought that the heavens were perfect and incorruptible. The very transient nature of comets seemed to imply that they were not part of the heavens but were merely earthly exhalations ignited and transported by heat to the upper atmosphere. Although the Roman philosopher Seneca (1st century CE) had proposed that comets could be heavenly bodies like the planets, Aristotle's ideas prevailed until the 14th century CE.

Finally, during the 16th century, the Danish nobleman Tycho Brahe established critical proof that comets are heavenly bodies. He compared the lack of diurnal parallax of the comet of 1577 with the well-known parallax of the Moon (the diurnal parallax is the apparent change of position in the sky relative to the distant stars due to the rotation of Earth). Tycho deduced that the comet was at least four times farther away than the Moon, establishing for the first time that comets were heavenly bodies.

In 1619, the German astronomer Johannes Kepler still believed in 1619 that comets travel across the sky in a straight line. It was the English physicist and mathematician Isaac Newton who demonstrated in his *Principia* (1687) that, if heavenly bodies are attracted by a central body (the Sun) in proportion to the inverse square of its distance, they must move along a conic section (circle, ellipse, parabola, or hyperbola). Using the observed positions of the Great Comet of 1680, he identified its orbit as being nearly parabolic.

MODERN RESEARCH

During the 19th century it was shown that the radiant (i.e., spatial direction) of the spectacular meteor showers of 1866, 1872, and 1885 coincided well with three known cometary orbits that happened by chance to cross Earth's orbit at the dates of the observed showers. The apparent relationship between comets and meteor showers was interpreted by assuming that the cometary nucleus was an aggregate of dust or sand grains without any cohesion, through a concept known as the "sand-bank" model. Meteor showers were explained by the spontaneous scattering of the dust grains along a comet's orbit, and the cometary nucleus began to be regarded only as the densest part of a meteor stream.

At the end of the 19th and the beginning of the 20th century, spectroscopy revealed that the reflection of sunlight by the dust was not the only source of light in the tail, showing the discontinuous emission that constitutes the signature of gaseous compounds. More specifically, it revealed the existence in the coma of several radicals— molecular fragments such as cyanogen (CN) and the carbon forms C_2 and C_3, which are chemically unstable in the laboratory because they are very reactive in molecular collisions. Spectroscopy also enabled investigators to detect the existence of a plasma component in the cometary tail by the presence of molecular ions, as, for example, those of carbon monoxide (CO^+), nitrogen (N_2^+), and carbon dioxide (CO_2^+). The radicals and ions are built up by the three light elements carbon (C), nitrogen (N), and oxygen (O). Hydrogen (H) was added when the radical CH was discovered belatedly on spectrograms of Comet Halley taken in 1910. The identification of CH was proposed by the American astronomer Nicholas Bobrovniko in 1931 and confirmed in 1938 by Marcel Nicolet of Belgium. In 1941 another Belgian astronomer, Pol Swings, and his coworkers identified three new ions: CH^+, OH^+, and CO_2^+. The emissions of the light elements hydrogen, carbon, oxygen, and sulfur and of carbon monoxide were finally detected when the far ultraviolet spectrum (which is absorbed by Earth's atmosphere) was explored during the 1970s with the help of rockets and satellites. This included the very large halo (10^7 km [62 million miles]) of atomic hydrogen (the Lyman-alpha emission line) first observed in Comets Tago-Sato-Kosaka 1969 IX and Bennett 1970 II.

Although the sandbank model was still seriously considered until the 1960s and '70s by a small minority (most notably the British astronomer Raymond A. Lyttleton), the presence of large amounts of gaseous fragments of volatile molecules in the coma suggested to Bobrovniko the release by the nucleus of a bulk of unobserved "parent" molecules such as H_2O, CO_2, and NH_3 (ammonia). In 1948, Swings proposed that these molecules should be present in the nucleus in the solid state as ices.

In a fundamental paper, the American astronomer Fred L. Whipple set forth in 1950 the so-called "dirty snowball" model, according to which the nucleus is a lumpy piece of icy conglomerate wherein dust is cemented by a large amount of ices—not only water ice but also ices of more volatile molecules. This amount must be substantial enough to sustain the vaporizations for a large number of revolutions. Whipple noted that the nuclei of some comets at least are solid enough to graze the Sun without experiencing total destruction, since they apparently survive unharmed. (Some but not all Sun-grazing nuclei split under solar tidal forces.)

Finally, argued Whipple, the asymmetric vaporization of the nuclear ices sunward produces a jet action opposite to the Sun on the solid cometary nucleus. When the nucleus is rotating, the jet action is not exactly radial. This explained the theretofore mysterious nongravitational force identified as acting on cometary orbits. In particular, the orbital period of 2P/Encke mysteriously decreased by one to three hours per revolution (of 3.3 years), whereas that of 1P/Halley increased by some three days per revolution (of 76 years). For Whipple, a prograde rotation of the nucleus of 2P/Encke and a retrograde rotation of that of 1P/Halley could explain these observations. In each case, a similar amount of some 0.5 to 0.25 percent of the ices had to be lost per revolution to explain the amount of the nongravitational force. Thus, all comets decay in a matter of a few hundred revolutions. This duration is only at most a few centuries for Encke and a few millennia for Halley. At any rate, it is millions of times shorter than the age of the solar system. However, comets are constantly replenished from the Kuiper Belt and the Oort cloud.

THE PROCESS OF DISCOVERY

Up to the beginning of the 19th century, comets were discovered exclusively by visual means. Many discoveries are still made visually with moderate-size telescopes by amateur astronomers. Although comets can be present in any region of the sky, they are often discovered near the western horizon after sunset or near the eastern horizon before sunrise, since they are brightest when closest to the Sun. Because of Earth's rotation and direction of motion in its orbit, discoveries before sunrise are more likely, as confirmed by discovery statistics.

At discovery a comet may still be faint enough not to have developed a tail; therefore, it may look like any nebulous object—e.g., an emission nebula, a globular star cluster, or a galaxy. The famous 18th-century French comet hunter Charles Messier (nicknamed "the ferret of comets" by Louis XV for his discovery of 21 comets) compiled his well-known catalog of "nebulous objects" so that such objects would not be mistaken for comets. The final criterion remains the apparent displacement of the comet after a few hours or a few days with respect to the distant stars; by contrast, the nebulous objects of Messier's catalog do not move. After such a displacement has been indisputably observed, any amateur wishing to have the comet named for himself must report his claim to the nearest observatory as soon as possible.

Most comets are and remain extremely faint. Today, a larger and larger proportion of comet discoveries are thus made fortuitously from high-resolution photographs, as, for instance, those taken during sky surveys by professional astronomers engaged in other projects. The faintest recorded comets approach the limit of detection of large telescopes (those that are 8 metres [26 feet] or more in diameter). Several successive observations of these faint moving objects are necessary to ensure identification and simultaneous calculation of a preliminary orbit. In order to determine a preliminary orbit as quickly as possible, the eccentricity $e = 1$ is assumed since some 90 percent of the observed eccentricities are close to one, and a parabolic motion is computed. This is generally sufficient to ensure against "losing" the comet in the sky.

The best conic section representing the path of the comet at a given instant is known as the osculating orbit. It is tangent to the true path of the chosen instant, and the velocity at that point is the same as the true instantaneous velocity of the comet. Nowadays, high-speed computers make it possible to produce a final ephemeris (table of positions) that is not only based on the definitive orbit but also includes the gravitational forces of the Sun and of all significant planets that constantly change the osculating orbit. In spite of this fact, the deviation between the observed and the predicted positions usually grows (imperceptibly) with the square of time. This is the signature of a "neglected" acceleration, which comes from a nongravitational force. Formulas representing the smooth variation of the nongravitational force with heliocentric distance are now included for many orbits. The most successful formula assumes that water ice prevails and controls the vaporization of the nucleus.

INSIDE COMETS

As previously noted, the traditional picture of a comet with a hazy head and a spectacular tail applies only to a transient phenomenon produced by the decay in the solar heat of a tiny object known as the cometary nucleus. In the largest telescopes, the nucleus is never more than a bright point of light at the centre of the cometary head. At substantial distances from the Sun, the comet seems to be reduced to its starlike nucleus. The nucleus is the essential part of a comet because it is the only permanent feature that survives during the entire lifetime of the comet. In particular, it is the source of the gases and dust that are released to build up the coma and tail when a comet approaches the Sun. The coma and tail are enormous: typically the coma measures a million km (621,371 miles) or more in diameter, and the tail may extend about 100 million km (62,137,119 miles) in length. They scatter and continuously dissipate into space but are steadily rebuilt by the decay of the nucleus, whose size is usually in the range of 10 km (6 miles).

The evidence on the nature of the cometary nucleus remained completely circumstantial until March 1986, when the first close-up photographs of the nucleus of Comet Halley were taken during a flyby by the Giotto spacecraft of the European Space Agency. Whipple's basic idea that the cometary nucleus was a monolithic piece of icy conglomerate had been already well supported by indirect deductions in the 1960s and '70s and had become the dominant though not universal view. The final proof of the existence of such a "dirty snowball," however, was provided by the photographs of Comet Halley's nucleus.

Composite image of Comet Wild 2's nucleus taken by the Stardust spacecraft during its 2004 flyby.

If there was any surprise, it was not over its irregular shape (variously described as a potato or a peanut), which had been expected for a body with such small gravity (10^{-4}g, where g is the gravity of Earth). Rather, it was over the very black colour of the nucleus, which suggests that the snows or ices are indeed mixed together with a large amount of soot-like materials (i.e., carbon and tar in ne dust form). The very low geometric albedo (2 to 4 percent) of the cometary nucleus puts it among the darkest objects of the solar system. Its size is thus somewhat larger than anticipated: the roughly elongated body measures 15 by 8 km (9 by 5 miles) and has a total volume of some 500 cubic km (120 cubic miles). Its mass is rather uncertain, estimated in the vicinity of 10^{17} grams, and its bulk density is very small, ranging anywhere from 0.1 to 0.8 g/cm³ (0.06 to 0.46 oz/in³). The infrared spectrometer on board the Soviet Vega 2 spacecraft estimated a surface temperature of 300 to 400 K for the inactive "crust" that seems to cover 90 percent of the nucleus. Whether this crust is only a warmer layer of outgassed dust or whether the dust particles are really fused together by vacuum welding under contact is still open to speculation.

The 10 percent of the surface of Halley's nucleus that shows signs of activity seems to correspond to two large and a few smaller circular features resembling volcanic vents. Large sunward jets of dust originate from the vents; they are clearly dragged away by the gases vaporizing from the nucleus. This vaporization has to be a sublimation of the ices that cools them down to no more than 200 K in the open vents. The chemical composition of the vaporizing gases, as expected, is dominated by water vapour (about 80 percent of the total production rate). The next most abundant volatile (close to 10 percent) appears to be carbon monoxide (CO), though it could come from the dissociation of another parent molecule (e.g., carbon dioxide [CO_2] or formaldehyde [CH_2O]). Following CO in abundance is CO_2 (close to 4 percent). Methane (CH_4) and ammonia (NH_3), on the other hand, seem to be close to the 0.5 to

1 percent level, and the percentage of carbon disulfide (CS_2) is even lower; at that level, there also must be unsaturated hydrocarbons and amino compounds responsible for the molecular fragments observed in the coma.

This is not identical to—though definitely reminiscent of—the composition of the volcanic gases on Earth, which also

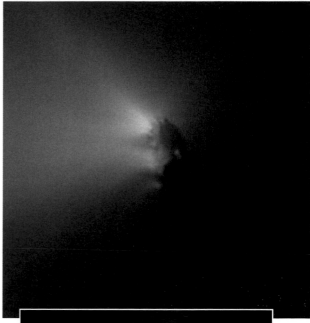

Composite image of the nucleus of Halley's Comet produced from 68 photographs taken from the Giotto spacecraft.

are dominated by water vapour. However, their CO_2:CO, CO_2:CH_4, and SO_2:S_2 ratios are all larger than in Comet Halley, meaning that the volcanic gases are more oxidized. The major difference may stem from the different temperature involved—often near 1,300 K in terrestrial volcanoes, as opposed to 200 K for cometary vaporizations. This may make the terrestrial gases closer to thermodynamic equilibrium. The dust-to-gas mass ratio is uncertain but is possibly in the vicinity of 0.4 to 1.1.

The dust grains are predominantly silicates. Mass spectrometric analysis by the Giotto spacecraft revealed that they contain as much as 20–30 percent carbon, which explains why they are so black. There also are grains composed almost entirely of organic material (molecules made of atoms of hydrogen, carbon, nitrogen, and oxygen).

There is some uncertainty concerning the rotation of Halley's nucleus. Two different rotation rates of 2.2 days and 7.3 days have been deduced by different methods. Both may exist, one of them involving a tumbling motion, or nutation, that results from the irregular shape of the nucleus, which has two quite different moments of inertia along perpendicular axes.

Scientific knowledge of the internal structure of the cometary nucleus was not enhanced by the flyby of Comet Halley, and so it rests on weak circumstantial evidence from the study of other comets. Earlier investigations had established that the outer layers of old comets were processed by solar heat. These layers must have lost most of their volatiles and developed a kind of outgassed crust, which probably measures a few metres in thickness. Inside the crust there is thought to exist an internal structure that is radially the same at any depth. Arguments supporting this view are based on the fact that cometary comas and tails do not become essentially different when comets decay. Since they lose more and more of their outer layers, however, the observed phenomena come from material from increasingly greater depths. These arguments are specifically concerned with the dust-to-gas mass ratio, the atomic and molecular spectra, the splitting rate, and the vaporization pattern during fragmentation.

Before the Giotto flyby of Comet Halley, other cometary nuclei had never been resolved optically. For this reason, their albedos had to be assumed first in order to compute their sizes. Techniques proposed to deduce the albedo yielded only that of the dusty nuclear region made artificially brighter by light scattering in the dust. In 1986 the albedo of Comet Halley's nucleus was found to be very low (2 to 4 percent). If this value is typical for other comets, then 11 of 18 short-period comets studied would be between 6 and 10 km (3 and 6 miles) in diameter; only 7 of them would be somewhat outside these limits. Comet Schwassmann-Wachmann 1 would be a giant with a diameter of 96 km; 10 long-period comets would all have diameters close to 16 km (59 miles; within 10 percent).

Since short-period comets have remained much longer in the solar system than comets having very long periods, the smaller size of the short-period comets might result from the steady fragmentation of the nucleus by splitting. Yet, the albedo may also diminish with aging. At the beginning, if the albedo were close to that of slightly less dirty snow (10 percent), the nuclear diameter of long-period comets would come very close to that of the largest of the short-period comets. The diameters of new comets also have been shown to be rather constant and most likely measure close to 10 km (6 miles). Of course, these are mean "effective" diameters of unseen bodies that are all likely to be very irregular.

The region around the nucleus, up to 10 or 20 times its diameter, contains an amount of dust large enough to be partially and irregularly opaque or at least optically thick. It scatters substantially more solar light than is reflected by the black nucleus. Dust jets develop mainly sunward, activated by the solar heat on the sunlit side of the nucleus. They act as a fountain that displaces somewhat the centre of light from the centre of mass of the nucleus. This region also is likely to contain large clusters of grains that have not yet completely decayed into finer dust; the grains are cemented together by ice.

THE TAIL OF THE COMET

The tails of comets are generally directed away from the Sun. They rarely appear beyond 1.5 or 2 AU but develop rapidly with shorter heliocentric distance. The onset of the tail near the nucleus is first directed toward the Sun and shows jets curving backward like a fountain, as if they were pushed by a force emanating from the Sun. The German astronomer Friedrich Wilhelm Bessel began to study this phenomenon in 1836, and Fyodor A. Bredikhin of Russia developed, in 1903, tail kinematics based on precisely such a repulsive force that varies as the inverse square of the distance to the Sun.

Halley's Comet, 1986.

Bredikhin introduced a scheme for classifying cometary tails into three types, depending on whether the repulsive force was more than 100 times the gravity of the Sun (Type I) or less than one solar gravity (Types II and III). Subsequent research showed that Type-I tails are plasma tails (containing observed molecular ions as well as electrons not visible from ground-based observatories), and Types II and III are dust tails, the differences between them being attributable to a minor difference in the size distribution of the dust grains. As a result of these findings, the traditional classification formulated by Bredikhin is no longer considered viable and is seldom used. Most comets (but not all) simultaneously show both types of tail: a bluish plasma tail, straight and narrow with twists and nods, and a yellowish dust tail, wide and curved, which is often featureless.

The plasma tail has its onset in a region extremely close to the nucleus. The ion source lies deep in the collision zone (typically 1,000 km [621 miles]). It is likely that charge-exchange reactions compete with the photoionization of parent molecules, but the mechanism that produces ions is not yet quantitatively understood. In 1951 the German astronomer Ludwig Biermann predicted the existence of the solar wind in order to account for the rapid accelerations observed in plasma tails as well as their aberration (i.e., deviation from the direction directly opposite the Sun). The cometary plasma is blown away by the magnetic field of the solar wind until it reaches its own velocity—nearly 400 km (248 miles) per second. This action explains the origin of the large forces postulated by the Bessel-Bredikhin theory. Spectacular changes observed in the plasma tail, such as its sudden total disconnection, have been explained by discontinuous changes in the solar wind flow (e.g., the passage of magnetic sector boundaries).

In 1957 the Swedish physicist Hannes Alfven predicted the draping of the magnetic lines of the solar wind around the cometary ionosphere. This phenomenon was detected by the International Cometary Explorer spacecraft, launched by the U.S. National Aeronautics and Space Administration (NASA), when it passed through the onset of the plasma tail of Comet 21P/Giacobini-Zinner on

September 11, 1985. Two magnetic lobes separated by a current-carrying neutral sheet were observed as expected. A related feature known as the ionopause was detected by the Giotto space probe during its flyby of Comet Halley in 1986. The ionopause is a cavity without a magnetic field that contains only cometary ions and is separated from the solar wind by a sharp discontinuity. Halley's ionopause lies about 4,000 to 5,000 km (2,500 to 3,100 miles) from the nucleus of the comet. An analysis of all the encounter data indicates that a complete understanding of cometary interaction with the solar wind has not yet been achieved. It is well understood, however, that the neutral coma remains practically spherical. The solar wind is so rarefied that there are no direct collisions of its particles with the neutral particles of the coma, and, as these particles are electrically neutral, they do not "feel" the magnetic field.

The source of the dust tail is the dust dragged away by the vaporizing gases that emanate from the active zones of the nucleus, presumably from vents like those observed on Comet Halley's nucleus. The dust jets are first directed sunward but are progressively pushed back by the radiation pressure of sunlight. The repulsive acceleration of a particle varies as $(sd)^{-1}$ (with linear size s and density d). For a given density, it thus varies as s^{-1}, separating widely the particles of different sizes in different parts of the tail. Studying the dust tail isophotes of varying brightnesses therefore yields the dust grain distribution. This distribution may peak for very ne particles near 0.5 micrometre (0.00002 inch), assuming a density of two, as in the case of Comet Bennett; however, it falls off with s^{-n} (with n ranging from three to five) for larger particles. This mechanism neglects particles much smaller than the mean wavelength of sunlight. Because such particles do not reflect light, they do not feel its radiation pressure. (They are not detected from ground-based observations anyway.)

One of the major results of the Giotto flyby of Halley's nucleus was the detection of abundant particles much smaller than the wavelength of light, indicating that the size distribution does not peak near 0.5 μm (0.00002 inch) but seems rather to grow indefinitely with a slope close to d^2 for finer and finer particles down to possibly 0.05 μm (10^{-17} gram). The dust composition analyzers on board the Giotto and Vega spacecraft revealed the presence of at least three broad classes of grains. Class 1 contains the light elements hydrogen, carbon, nitrogen, and oxygen only (in the form of either ices or polymers of organic compounds). The particles of class 2 are analogous to the meteorites known as CI carbonaceous chondrites but are possibly slightly enriched in carbon and sulfur. Class 3 particles are even more enriched in carbon, nitrogen, and sulfur; they could be regarded as carbonaceous silicate cores (like those of class 2) covered by a mantle of organic material (similar to that of class 1) that has been radiation-processed. Most of the encounter data were excellent for elemental analyses but poor for determining molecular composition, because most molecules were destroyed by impact at high encounter velocity. Hence, there still remains much ambiguity regarding the chemical nature of the organic fraction present in the grains.

Meteors are extraterrestrial particles of sand-grain or small-pebble size that become luminous upon entering the upper atmosphere at very high speeds. Meteor streams have well-defined orbits in space. More than a dozen of these orbits have practically the same orbital elements as the orbits of the identical number of short-period comets. Fine cometary dust consists primarily of micrometre- or sub-micrometre-size particles that are much too small to become visible meteors (they are more like cigarette smoke than dust). Moreover, they are scattered in the cometary tail at great distance from the comet orbit. The size distribution of cometary dust grains, however, covers many orders of magnitude; a small fraction of them may reach 0.1 millimetre (0.004 inch) to even a few centimetres. Because of their large size, these dust grains are almost not accelerated by the radiation pressure of sunlight. They remain in the plane of the cometary orbit and in the immediate vicinity of the orbit itself, even though they separate steadily from the nucleus.

They sometimes become visible as an anti-tail—i.e., as a bright spike extending from the coma sunward in a direction opposite to the tail. This phenomenon occurs as a matter of geometry: it takes place for only a few days when Earth crosses the plane of the cometary orbit. At such a time, this plane is viewed through the edge, and all large grains are seen accumulated along a line. The same grains scatter farther and farther away from the nucleus until some are along the entire cometary orbit. When Earth's orbit intersects such an orbit (an event that occurs year after year at the same calendar date), these large grains produce meteor showers.

Extremely fine cometary grains also may penetrate Earth's atmosphere, but they can be slowed down gently without burning up. Some have been collected by NASA's U-2 aircraft at very high altitudes. Grains of this kind are known as Brownlee particles and are believed to be of cometary origin. Their composition is chondritic, though they show somewhat more carbon and sulfur than the CI carbonaceous chondrites. Similar grains were found in space during the space probe exploration of Comet Halley.

ORIGIN AND EVOLUTION

All observed comets make up an essentially transient system that decays and disappears almost completely in less than one million years. Since they all pass through the solar system, planetary perturbations eject a fraction of them into deep space on hyperbolic orbits and capture another fraction on short-period orbits. In turn, those that have been captured decay rapidly in the solar heat. Fortunately, there is a permanent source of new comets that maintains the steady state—namely, the outer margin of the Oort cloud. Comets within the bulk of the Oort cloud are unobservable, not only because they do not develop comas and tails but also because they are too far away.

Any modern theory about cometary origins has to consider the origin of the Oort cloud. None of the comets observed today left the Oort cloud more than three or four million years ago. The Oort cloud is, however, gravitationally bound to the solar system, which it follows in its orbit around the Milky Way Galaxy. Therefore, it is likely that the Oort cloud has existed for a long time. The most probable hypothesis is that it was formed at the same time as the giant planets by the very process that accreted them. The Soviet astronomer Viktor S. Safronov developed this accretionary theory of planetary system mathematically in 1972. According to his model, the planets originated from a disk or a ring of dust around the Sun, and cometary nuclei are nothing more than primordial planetesimals that accreted first and became the building blocks of the planets. From the accreted mass of the giant planets,

HALLEY'S COMET

Halley's Comet was the first comet whose return was predicted and, almost three centuries later, the first to be photographed up close by spacecraft. In 1705 the English astronomer Edmond Halley published a work that included his calculations showing that comets observed in 1531, 1607, and 1682 were really one comet and predicting that comet's return in 1758. The comet was sighted late in 1758, passed perihelion (closest distance to the Sun) in March 1759, and was named in Halley's honour.

Dozens of earlier passages of Halley's Comet were later calculated and checked against historical records of comet sightings. Its earliest recorded appearance, witnessed by Chinese astronomers, was in 240 BCE. Its closest approach to Earth took place in April 837. It was the large, bright comet seen during the Norman Conquest of England (1066) and shown in the Bayeux Tapestry of that time. Its passage in 1301 appears to have inspired the form of the Star of Bethlehem that the Italian painter Giotto used in his "The Adoration of the Magi." Its passages have taken place about 76 years apart on average, but the gravitational influence of the planets on the comet's orbit have caused the orbital period to vary by a year or two from one reappearance to the next. During the comet's return in 1910, Earth probably passed through part of its tail, which was millions of kilometres in length, with no apparent effect.

As predicted, the comet passed Earth in November–December 1985, reached perihelion on February 9, 1986, and came closest to Earth on April 11, 1986. Its passage was observed by two Japanese spacecraft (Sakigake and Suisei), two Soviet spacecraft (Vega 1 and Vega 2), and a European Space Agency spacecraft (Giotto). Close-up images of the comet's nucleus made by Giotto show an oblong object with dimensions of about 15 × 8 km (9 × 5 miles). Dust particles shed during the comet's slow disintegration over the millennia are distributed along its orbit. The passage of Earth through this debris stream every year is responsible for the Orionid and Eta Aquarid meteor showers in October and May, respectively.

Halley's Comet is next expected to return to the inner solar system in 2061.

Safronov predicted the correct order of magnitude of the mass of the Oort cloud, which was built up by those planetesimals that missed colliding with the planetary embryos and were thrust far away by their perturbations. In effect, the Oort cloud in this theory becomes the necessary consequence and the natural by-product of the accretion of the giant planets.

Later, in the 1970s, the American astronomer A.G.W. Cameron developed a much more massive model of the protostar nebula, in which the comets accreted in a circular ring at some 1,000 AU from the Sun, which is far beyond the present limits of the planetary system. The primeval circular orbits were then transformed into the elongated ellipses present in the Oort cloud by mass loss of the primitive solar nebula. Both the Cameron and Safronov models put the origin of comets together with that of the solar system some 4.6 billion years ago. Plausibility is given to the general idea of accretion from dust disks by the existence of such disks around many young stars—a fact established by infrared observations in the 1980s and confirmed visually in at least one case (β Pictoris). Further support is found in clues derived from meteorites.

Since the early 1980s, new ideas have been explored to determine whether the Oort cloud could be much younger than the solar system or at least periodically replenished. The role of the massive and dense molecular clouds that exist in interstellar space has been reexamined in different ways. Could comets have accreted in these clouds directly from interstellar grains? Mechanisms for later capturing them into the Oort cloud cannot be very effective, but the efficiency is not capital, and some possibilities have been proposed. Since the solar system itself was probably formed from the gravitational collapse of such a molecular cloud, it seems more likely that either comets or the interstellar grains that were going to accrete into comets followed suit during gaseous collapse and were put into the Oort cloud at the same time that the planets were being formed. Elemental isotopic ratios deduced from the Comet Halley flyby have not brought about any conspicuous anomalies that could be attributed to matter coming from outside the solar system. So far, observational clues all favour the idea of cometary matter deriving from the same primeval reservoir as the stuff of the solar system, but it must be recognized that the evidence remains weak.

Telltales based on the chemical constitution of cometary nuclei as well as on the evolution of their orbits suggest that the origin of comets goes back beyond that of the planets and their satellites. Two scenarios are among the likeliest possibilities. In the first, comets had already accreted in all dense molecular clouds of the Milky Way Galaxy by the agglomeration of interstellar grains covered by a frost of organic molecules that cemented them together. Later, such a cloud collapsed to form the solar system. In the second scenario, dense molecular clouds were not able to accrete their frosty interstellar grains into larger bodies. When one of these molecular clouds collapsed to form the future solar system, however, the interstellar grains did likewise and eventually formed a dusty disk around the central star—the proto-Sun. Accretion into objects of 10 km (6.2 mile) diameter is more likely in dusty disks of this type. The outer grains of the disk had not lost their frost, and some of them were ejected into the Oort cloud during the accretion of planetesimals into giant planets after some very moderate processing by heat. It is hoped that one day, space probes will secure data that will make it possible to determine whether frosty interstellar grains have lost their identity or can still be recognized as pristine and unaltered objects in cometary dust.

Comets seem to be the most pristine objects of the solar system, containing intact the material from which they were formed. Included are the hydrogen, carbon, oxygen, nitrogen, and sulfur atoms needed to build the volatile molecules present in the terrestrial biosphere (including the oceans and the atmosphere). Comets also seem to be the link between interstellar molecules and the most primitive meteorites known—the carbonaceous chondrites. The molecules required to initiate prebiotic chemistry (e.g., hydrogen cyanide, methyl cyanide, water, and formaldehyde) are present in interstellar space just as they are in comets; larger prebiotic chemistry molecules (e.g., amino acids, purines, and pyrimidines) occur in some chondrites and possibly in comets. An early cometary bombardment of Earth, predicted in some accretion models of the solar system, may have brought the oceans and the atmosphere, as well as a veneer of the molecules needed for life to develop on Earth. Comets could well be the link between interstellar chemistry and life.

Beyond our planet, Earth, and the other terrestrial planets—scorched Mercury, enshrouded Venus, and frigid Mars—lie the rocky bodies of the asteroid belt. If you look long enough at the night sky, eventually you will see a shooting star. This glowing streak is a meteor, and its cause is a relatively small stony or metallic natural object from space called a meteoroid that enters Earth's atmosphere and heats to incandescence. In ancient times, the regularity of the sky was a bedrock of stability in a harsh world. The Sun rose and set. The planets moved along the zodiac. However, sometimes, something new and frightening appeared, a star with a tail trailing behind it, a comet.

Since ancient times, astronomers have observed each of these celestial bodies—asteroids, meteors, meteorites, and comets—with wonder and curiosity. Today, with advances in technology, these once-mysterious objects are no longer mythology. Scientists can study them up close. They can analyze their composition and behaviour and understand their origins. Often, these celestial bodies are messengers from the distant past and the far reaches of space, giving us insight into the origins and nature of our solar system.

GLOSSARY

Cretaceous Of, relating to, or being the last period of the Mesozoic era, characterized by continued dominance of reptiles, emergent dominance of angiosperms, diversification of mammals, and the extinction of many types of organisms at the close of the period.

density The mass of a unit volume of a material substance.

extraterrestrial Originating, existing, or occurring outside Earth or its atmosphere.

friction The force that resists relative motion between two bodies in contact.

Kuiper Belt A band of small celestial bodies beyond the orbit of Neptune from which many short-period comets are believed to originate.

interstellar Something that is located, taking place, or traveling among the stars.

mass The property of a body that is a measure of its inertia and that is commonly taken as a measure of the amount of material it contains and causes it to have weight in a gravitational field.

nebula A mass of interstellar gas and dust.

nova A star that brightens temporarily while ejecting a shell explosively.

nucleosynthesis The production of a chemical element from simpler nuclei (as of hydrogen), especially in a star.

nucleus The small bright body in the head of a comet.

Oort cloud A spherical shell of cometary bodies believed to surround the Sun far beyond the orbits of the outermost planets and from which some are dislodged when perturbed to fall toward the sun.

orbit A path described by one body in its revolution about another.

planetesimal Any of numerous small celestial bodies that may have existed at an early stage of the development of the solar system.

seismometer A seismograph measuring the actual movements of the ground (as on Earth or the Moon).

silicate A salt or ester derived from a silicic acid from the Sun's surface.

solar wind Plasma continuously ejected from the Sun's surface into and through interplanetary space.

spectroscopy The production and investigation of spectra, a continuum of color formed when a beam of white light is dispersed.

tidal force The effect of the stretching of a body toward the center of mass of another body due to the gradient in strength of the gravitational field.

velocity The rate of change of position along a straight line with respect to time.

BIBLIOGRAPHY

THE UNIVERSE OF COMETS

General introductory works are John C. Brandt and Robert D. Chapman, *Introduction to Comets*, 2nd ed. (2003, reissued 2005); Jacques Crovisier and Thérèse Encrenaz, *Comet Science: The Study of Remnants From the Birth of the Solar System*, trans. from the French by Stephen Lyle (2000); Armand H. Delsemme, "Whence Come Comets?" *Sky and Telescope*, 77(3):260-264 (March 1989), an elementary discussion on their origin; Fred L. Whipple and Daniel W.E. Green, *The Mystery of Comets* (1985); and Robert D. Chapman and John C. Brandt, *The Comet Book: A Guide for the Return of Halley's Comet* (1984), a historical treatment. Brian G. Marsden and Gareth V. Williams, *Catalogue of Cometary Orbits*, 16th ed. (2005), covers 2,221 cometary orbits, with detailed references and notes; a complementary work is Gary W. Kronk, *Cometography: A Catalog of Comets*, 2 vol. (1999–2003). More-advanced works are R.L. Newburn, Jr., M. Neugebauer, and J. Rahe (eds.), *Comets in the Post-Halley Era*, 2 vol. (1991), containing reviews, summaries, and scientific papers by about one hundred authors; and K.S. Krishna Swamy, *Physics of Comets*, 2nd ed. (1997). Donald K. Yeomans, *Comets: A Chronological History of Observation, Science, Myth, and Folklore* (1991), is a comprehensive reference book on all cometary apparitions, full of anecdotes and highly recommended.

AMAZING ASTEROIDS

Summary articles about asteroids can be found in Richard P. Binzel, M. Antonietta Barucci, and Marcello Fulchignoni, "The Origins of the Asteroids," *Scientific American*, 265(4):88–94 (October 1991); and Clark R. Chapman, "Asteroids," in J. Kelly Beatty, Carolyn C. Petersen, and Andrew Chaikin (eds.), *The New Solar System*, 4th ed. (1999), pp. 337–350. Review and research papers are collected in Richard P. Binzel, Tom Gehrels, and Mildred Shapley Matthews (eds.), *Asteroids II*(1989); C.-I. Lagerkvist et al. (eds.), *Asteroids, Comets, Meteors III* (1990); Tom Gehrels (ed.), *Hazards Due to Comets & Asteroids* (1994); Alan W. Harris and Edward Bowell (eds.), *Asteroids, Comets, Meteors 1991* (1992); Andrea Milani, Mario Di Martino, and Alberto Cellino (eds.), *Asteroids, Comets, Meteors 1993* (1994); William F. Bottke, Jr., et al. (eds.), *Asteroids III* (2002); and Daniela Lazzaro, Sylvio Ferraz-Mello, and Julio A. Fernández (eds.), *Asteroids, Comets, and Meteors* (2006).

SHOOTING STARS: THE SCIENCE OF METEORS

Edmond Murad and Iwan P. Williams (eds.), *Meteors in the Earth's Atmosphere: Meteoroids and Cosmic Dust and*

Their Interactions with the Earth's Upper Atmosphere (2002), provides a comprehensive overview of the matter that falls to Earth from space. Peter Jenniskens, *Meteor Showers and Their Parent Comets* (2006), explains the origin of meteor streams and describes all known meteor showers, with particular attention given to the most important showers and their parent comets. Introductory information on meteorites and their relationship to meteoroids and asteroids can be found in Brigitte Zanda and Monica Rotaru (eds.), *Meteorites: Their Impact on Science and History* (2001; originally published in French, 1996); Alex Bevan and John de Laeter, *Meteorites: A Journey Through Space and Time* (2002); and Harry Y. McSween, Jr., *Meteorites and Their Parent Planets*, 2nd ed. (1999).

STUDYING METEORITES

Introductory information can be found in Brigitte Zanda and Monica Rotaru (eds.), *Meteorites: Their Impact on Science and History* (2001; originally published in French, 1996); Alex Bevan and John de Laeter, *Meteorites: A Journey through Space and Time* (2002); Harry Y. McSween, Jr., *Meteorites and Their Parent Planets*, 2nd ed. (1999); O. Richard Norton, *Rocks from Space: Meteorites and Meteorite Hunters*, 2nd ed. (1998); and Fritz Heide and

Frank Wlotzka, *Meteorites: Messengers from Space* (1995). More-advanced treatments are John T. Wasson, *Meteorites: Their Record of Early Solar-System History* (1985); V.A. Bronshten, *Physics of Meteoric Phenomena* (1983; originally published in Russian, 1981); and Robert Hutchison, *Meteorites: A Petrologic, Chemical, and Isotopic Synthesis* (2004). Dante S. Lauretta and Marvin Killgore, *A Color Atlas of Meteorites in Thin Section* (2005), provides a comprehensive collection of often-striking photographs of petrologic thin sections of meteorites. A descriptive and historical treatment of iron meteorites, including beautiful photographs, is Vagn F. Buchwald, *Handbook of Iron Meteorites, Their Distribution, Composition, and Structure*, 3 vol. (1975). H.H. Nininger, *Out of the Sky: An Introduction to Meteorites* (1952, reprinted 1959), provides firsthand experiences of fall phenomena on a nontechnical level. A catalog of known meteorites to the end of 1999, including data regarding their fall, is M.M. Grady (ed.), *Catalogue of Meteorites*, 5th ed. (2000).

INDEX

A

achondrites, 61, 65–69, 74

albedos, 25, 26, 71–72, 97, 101–102

Amor asteroids, 17–20

Apollo asteroids, 19–21, 23, 30–31

asteroid belt, 10, 16, 25–26, 31, 67, 81–83

asteroids
classification, 25–26, 72–74
meteorites and, 71–78
naming of, 16–17
near-Earth asteroids (NEAs), 17–24
19th-century observations of, 11–14
origin, 31–33
overview, 6–8, 10–11
rotation and shape, 26–27
spacecraft exploration of, 27–31
20th-century observations of, 14–16

B

Bessel-Bredikhin theory, 103–104

C

Ceres, 13, 16, 22, 31

chondrites, 61–63, 72, 74–75, 78, 81, 114–115

chondrules, 63, 81–82

comas, 24, 86–87, 96, 100, 105, 108

comets
classification, 87–88
compared to asteroids, 24–25
early study of, 89–90
meteor showers and, 44–46
modern research on, 90–95
nuclei of, 85–87, 90, 92–93, 95–102, 101, 105–108, 111
origin, 108–115
overview, 6–9, 24, 85–87, 96–102
tails of, 24, 85, 87, 96, 102–108

D

density, calculating, 22–23

E

Earth, asteroids close to, 17–24

Eros, 27–28, 72, 74–75